In Spite Of

SHIRLEY I. KISS

Order this book online at www.trafford.com
or email orders@trafford.com

Most Trafford titles are also available at major online book retailers.

Printed in the United States of America.

ISBN: 978-1-4669-5437-3 (sc)
ISBN: 978-1-4669-5438-0 (e)

Trafford rev. 10/04/2012

 www.trafford.com

North America & international
toll-free: 1 888 232 4444 (USA & Canada)
phone: 250 383 6864 ♦ fax: 812 355 4082

A PRELUDE

THERE ONCE WAS a woman named Rose, she loved her name. Rose. Rose Neumayer to be exact. She'd always claimed to have "no middle name" but in years to come she would 'confess' to it being Nathalia, which her granddaughters found endearing. She was born on the fourth of July in the year of 1900, in Chicago, Illinois. Her mother died on the seventh of July, when she was but three days old.

Soon, her father remarried and she and her brothers, Mathias, born August 12, 1896 and Lawrence, the following year, Theresa, the year after that, found they were part of a family of twelve siblings! Because she was the eldest girl, she was forced to leave school to "help" at home. She never got past the fourth grade, knowing only how to read and write and 'do' numbers. What she had much knowledge in though, was how to clean a house properly. Her step-mother made sure of that, and her brothers often teamed up to help 'educate' her as well. There was the time she had become frustrated and said: "Oh nuts!" when one of them dirtied up an area she had just cleaned, knowing she would be forced to re-do the floor. In a flash they picked her up and literally threw her down the basement stairs for 'talking dirty' (saying the word: 'nuts'). Her step-mother had little time to interfere with these actions, being actively involved in bearing children. With only one sister and two brothers of the same parents, no one stood up for her, so when the opportunity came to leave via marriage, she was happy. Even though it had been arranged by her father who received a dowry for her, she still felt it was an escape. The man she married was a strapping six foot tall window trimmer, she was a tiny girl of 5'2". Although she had willingly married to escape abuse she soon found herself trapped in yet another abusive situation. After giving birth to a baby girl, still in bed recovering, her husband brought a young woman into his bed. When Rose discovered this she of course, told her husband she wouldn't live like that and received a sound beating for her trouble. When she finally sought a divorce she lost custody of her daughter, Rosemary, because she had sought the divorce and it was, after all, the 1900's. Rosemary had become a victim of what was then known as Infantile Paralysis, later termed polio, and was confined to a wheelchair until the time of her death before reaching her teens. Rose's husband claimed she would be unable to care for a child and hold down a job. The mere fact that she did not 'obey' her husband was reason enough for the court system to condemn her, as did society at large. She got a job at Woolworth's five and dime store, in order to support herself. With so little formal education she was grateful for anything!

And then . . . . Love came to Rose!

Everett Voss was born, one of twin boys on December 20th, 1891 in Chicago, Illinois. his father was Louis John Voss, born in Hamburg, Germany, his mother Matilda (Tillie) Kull was born in St. Louis, Missouri. There were three other siblings at the time of his birth, only one of which he kept in touch with in his adult life. Not his twin, Roy, but his older brother, Olin. Everett had married at a young age as well, and fathered a son on September 16th, 1920, named after him. Soon illness overcame his wife, Katherine, and he found himself a widower in his early thirties. His two sisters-in-law who lived together, willingly took over caring for the boy.

One day, as he walked through the local five and dime store seeking a small gift for them and his young son, he decided to purchase some fudge. There, behind the counter, we find Rose. They talked some over the transaction as he explained it was a small token for his sisters in law's who cared for his young son while he worked.

It became a habit for him to return most every week and in time they formed a friendship. Soon an attraction on both sides was apparent and they began to see one another outside of her job. After some time, they became man and wife on June 30, 1926. His sisters in law thought this was scandalous behavior and told him so frequently. Marrying again was one thing, but to a divorced woman? Shameful! They began finding excuses why he couldn't see the boy, which he accepted for a time. But then it became painfully clear the youngsters' mind was being poisoned against his father. So began a long, legal fight for him to rightfully claim his son. This was accomplished when young Everett was nearly 6 years old. During this time Rose had become pregnant and was having a very difficult time. The last couple of months she was bedridden and quite weak. Finally, on May 29th, 1928 she gave birth to a baby girl. Whether the difficult pregnancy caused it or not, the child was pronounced dead and taken away as the doctor's worked on Rose. However, sometime later the child had begun to breathe on her own and regained a healthy color. After nearly two weeks mother and child were released but Rose remained bedridden for sometime before she regained her strength. Because it was believed then, that an infant should be baptized before any outing, and Rose had appointed her brother Lawrence and his wife, Irene as God-Parents, they and Everett went to the Church. On being presented to the priest they were all stunned to be informed that the names: "Shirley May" were not Catholic names! Irene quickly suggested her name be the middle name, and Everett, desperate to get this done agreed. So Shirley Irene Voss was baptized much to the chagrin of Rose when she was told. Refusing to accept the change of her decision, she insisted to everyone that Shirley's middle name was May, and in fact, entered her into school that way. Later, there would be repercussions because of that decision.

During this time, with so much drama around him, young Everett learned to cope by staying out of everyone's way. Inside though, he was angry at having been torn from his two maiden aunts who had doted on him. He felt left out now, dealing with a new baby which was being pampered due to her having survived. Everyone seemed occupied with his sickly stepmother which added to the lack of attention he wanted and felt he deserved. After all, he was only a boy of eight, it just didn't seem fair to him at all. Soon he began to act out his feelings in many ways. And the future didn't look quite as bright to Everett and Rose.

SHIRLEY IRENE

In The Beginning

AS SHIRLEY LEFT babyhood, so did the family leave their neighborhood. Living near the Chicago River, often times Rose would push her in her buggy, across the bridge, where one day, so the story went, baby Shirley tossed her mother's purse through the rails and into the river! The family had a large collie dog, named Lad, who used to watch over baby Shirley as though she were one of his pups. Many times, went yet another story of her baby-hood, Lad would grab Shirley by her dress, and drag her across the grass to keep her away from any traffic! Many Sunday afternoon's they would accompany another family to Navy Pier. Having formed a friendship with the captain of one of the huge ships that docked and offered rides into Lake Michigan, Lad was given to him.

The move found them in a lovely bungalow on Keeler Avenue, two blocks from the main street car line, Fullerton Avenue. Everett was sent to the nearby Catholic school, while Shirley remained home, too young for school. The next door neighbors were an elderly couple, named Nick and Mary. Coming from the "old country" (Italy), they spoke very little English but were always kind to her as she played in the backyard. One day Mary passed away and Shirley was taken into their parlor where Mary lay in her casket with lit candles on either side. Though she felt no fear, Shirley always remembered that somber scene. Because there were no little children nearby, she was fairly much left alone to amuse herself in whatever fashion. There was a sandbox under the enclosed porch and many an hour she spent there. She was also allowed to play with the garden hose, which she frequently did, making mud pies, decorated with berries from the bushes in their yard.

Shirley had her own bedroom, across the hall from her parents, Everett, however had his bed in the attic. He used to make balsam-wood airplanes by the hour and had them hanging from all the rafters. On rare occasions Shirley would be allowed to go up there and was always enthralled with all the space he had, and how he kept it decorated with these planes. On weekdays they would all eat in the kitchen, but on special days they would use the dining room. Shirley loved sitting in there, it was so pretty! On days like Thanksgiving or Christmas she and Everett were both given small glasses of wine as well. She was always treated well, as far back as she could remember. One memory she had of Everett as a young boy was when he was making lead soldiers. He used molten lead and somehow had spilled it onto his inner arm. In great pain, and fearful of being "caught" he had immersed his arm under the faucet in the kitchen sink, and who should discover him, but Shirley! Running into the other room to her parents she announced that "the boy" had a big owie! Rose came into the kitchen and took in the situation, she simply told him to dry himself off, and get up to his room! There would be no more lead soldiers for him! He was never taken to a doctor, and all his life he carried horrendous scars up and down that arm! Everett never stood up for his son, even though he had fought for his custody, and though she was young Shirley must have picked up on those vibes, for Everett told her she was a wicked little tattle tale! Somehow, the two were raised in the same house yet never knew one another as brother and sister. Because Everett was difficult for a little one to say, she simply called him "boy"! The eight year difference in their ages did not keep Everett from resenting the love of attention she received and would often retaliate by doing small but cruel things to her. He would put pins in a rubber ball then offer to "play catch" with her. When the pins pricked her hands and she would cry out with pain he would simply scoop up the ball quickly, remove the pins, and state innocently he had no idea why she was such a cry baby! Yet, there were other times, especially as she grew older, when he would display affection for her, in spite of himself! Many times he would hoist her up on his shoulder and get her to church, it being such a long walk. Neither Everett nor Rose attended mass, but were insistent that the two children should. As he continued to act out his rebellion he was ejected from parochial school for "behavior problems", (throwing spitballs at the nun for one thing!) so he went to public school for the remainder of his grade schooling.

Often, in the evening, Everett and Rose would walk down to the "corner tavern", at which time Everett and Shirley were left alone. Later in life she was to learn that after their parents left, so did Everett! He had a rope rigged up, wrapped around the chimney, so that he could leave through the attic window! It seems that they had locked the door to the attic, with a towel around the knob, so it could be told if he'd come downstairs. So he simply outsmarted them. Perhaps it was just as well little Shirley never knew how frequently she was left alone, sleeping, in that bungalow! By time she turned 5, in 1933, she too, entered Barry School. The two were able to walk together for a time, and then Everett went on to Kelvyn Park High School. School was an amazing world for Shirley. She learned to read, the most wonderful gift of all! She made friends throughout the years there, graduating in 1942. During that period she learned so much about so many things. She ate her lunch at the school store across the street, with other youngsters who lived too far away to go home. The school had no lunchroom, but they did have a large gym which was a glorious place to play and run off steam in. In seventh and eighth grades they were able to play music and have dances, where both boys and girls were taught the art of ballroom dancing. What fun!

Meanwhile, back at the house things were about to change once again. It seemed, they were told, that "we are moving." It would be their job to "get rid of anything they didn't really need" because the place they were moving to, was much smaller than the bungalow. The place turned out to be an upstairs, rear apartment, the front apartment was above a tavern, and the owners lived there. The downstairs rear apartment was rented by an elderly Polish couple. There were three bedrooms, but they were very small, yet both Shirley and Everett did have their own rooms. This move also meant another three blocks added to Shirley's walk to school, the

High School was closer for Everett. Still she begged her father to allow her to finish her schooling at Barry, because she knew no-one at the closer Nixon School. Somehow he did manage to get her a permit so she could do so. They were right on the corner of Tripp, one block over from Keeler, and Fullerton. The streetcar stopped right on their corner. Shirley was thrilled to be where there was so much more activity! She would spend much time, sitting at the kitchen table, gazing out on the streets, people watching! Everyone, it seemed, had some place to go, and they were all walking there, past her window! Being on the second floor also allowed her to look without anyone being able to look back at her. When her mother would send her out to the grocer or meat market or drugstore, she enjoyed being able to do these errands, to walk among so many others. Mostly, she loved going to the meat market, with the sawdust on the floor, and the huge pickle barrels set out. Sometimes, mother would allow her to spend two cents and buy one of those huge dill pickles! Her mother told her how when she was young, she and her friends would stick peppermint or lemon sticks into a large dill pickle and suck the juice up. Sure sounded disgusting, but once she tried it, she and her friends used to do the same thing.

While there had never been any sign of physical abuse, there were no real signs of affection either, even between Rose and Everett. A simple kiss goodbye each morning as he left for work, and again on his return. Then, when Shirley was about 10 years old she witnessed what would be a final confrontation between her father and Everett. He had been in and out of trouble for most of his teen years, both in and out of school. By the time he had reached his senior year the quarrels between him and his father escalated. In her bedroom reading, one evening she heard loud voices. Soon the loudness became actual shouting. Recognizing her father and brothers' voices she threw open her door and watched in shock, as her father continued his tirade right in Everett's face. Because she had come to know the good side of Everett she very much felt the need to go to his defense, yet was fearful to do so. Still, she slowly ventured from her bedroom and was surprised to hear herself shout: "No, No, don't . . .", but was cut off by her father as he told her to go back in her room. Afraid to not mind, yet she hovered outside the doorway shaking and frightened, knowing this particular argument was far more serious than any she'd witnessed before. Suddenly she saw her father punch

Everett—not once, but several times—and with a fist! Her father was but 5'1",
slightly overweight, with an extended stomach from the beer he consumed. Her
brother, in contrast, stood at 5'9" and was young and strong from all the task's
he'd been made to perform over the years, including carting around a sister. But
there he stood, solidly, with one arm in front of his face for protection only. Not
once did he try to defend himself by striking out. Rather, he gave that sad, tight
little grin she'd seen so often, and simply said: "I'm going!" Looking toward Rose,
he added: "That's what SHE has wanted all along, and seems that's what you want
too." Losing all control, Shirley ran to the kitchen doorway trying to reach out to
Everett, but was held back by her father. Tears streaming down her face, as she
tried to twist away from her father's grip on her wrist, she begged him not to let
her brother go. Shoving her backward into her mother, he leaned over the second
floor railing and shouted at Everett's back: "GO! Go ahead and go, you'll come
crawling back or end up in jail where you belong!" Coming back into the kitchen
he slammed the door shut and strode angrily into the front room.

Shirley spent that night lying in her bed crying and praying that God would watch
over Everett, unaware that her own words ('my brother') had added even more fuel
to her father's anger. In the morning when she tried to approach her mother about
what had happened, her mother's response was that she didn't want to discuss
it—ever. If she knew what was good for her Shirley would not bring it up again.
Besides, she was informed, it was none of her business anyway, after all Everett
was her husband's son nothing to her or to Shirley! Still, rebelling at her mother's
attitude, she slowly and somewhat fearfully approached her father that evening.
She begged him to reconsider, to take Everett back home, but was stunned by his
cruel response. She was told: "Forget Everett! He was never anything to you, he is
not your brother! He is nothing! He has done nothing but cause trouble between
your mother and I all these years. What happened—happened. It is now done
and over with. Do you understand young lady? Don't you ever—EVER mention
him around her again!" Once again using the newspaper as his barrier, he simply
ignored her presence. This was an awakening for her, however shocking, she had
to accept the fact her parents could be really cruel people. What an eye opening
fact for a young girl to try to accept. She found herself mulling over this change of

circumstance many times when she was alone. She tried to understand how it had all come about, and where it left her!

The next day, when she returned from school she was surprised to find her mother home, and so she was able to enter the apartment. Never having been able to enter their home when a parent was not present, had never happened, usually she had to sit on the stairs in the hallway until her mother returned. Even in the bungalow she never had access to the house, although she wore a house key on a string around her neck, it only opened the door of the enclosed porch, not the house proper. So, she entered slowly, wondering what had brought about this particular change. As she neared Everett's room, heading toward her own bedroom, she encountered her mother on the way out of his room. She stood there in the doorway with what seemed to Shirley a strange sort of smile on her face. Peering over her mothers shoulder Shirley was shocked to see that Everett's room no longer existed! All his belongings were gone, and the room had undergone a big cleaning and a complete overhaul! Continuing on into her own room, she wondered what now?! "What is going on now?" She would find out, within a week, what was going on. Meantime, Shirley found it strange that no one ever asked about Everett, no one seemed to notice he was gone! She realized that they were new to the neighborhood, but still, shouldn't someone question the fact that Everett was no longer living there?! But no one ever did.

Then, once a week had gone by, Shirley was informed as to her silent question of: "What now?!" Once again, on returning home from school, Shirley found the door unlocked, and on entering the kitchen she found her mother sitting at the table talking quietly with a strange man. Shirley was informed that this was Dick, their 'roomer', who would be staying in the 'extra room'. ("Everett's room" thought Shirley soundlessly) and nodding she went on to her room. Afraid to question this whole new change of events she simply accepted it, and stayed in her room more than ever. Having been told to "do as your told, and mind your mother" so imprinted in her mind, what else could she do?

When she was about to turn 13, she sought to find a job during summer vacation, only to be told she would need a work permit. She had so looked forward to having money of her own, other than the couple dollars she earned from occasional babysitting for neighbors. Although her mother supplied her with clothing, she was never allowed to choose anything and she yearned to dress as her schoolmates did. Gathering up her courage she asked her mother for her birth certificate so she might obtain the permit. Her mother was not at all pleased with the idea, she was willing to let Shirley work, but wasn't sure she could be trusted with such an important paper, after all she was rather stupid and not the most dependable. However, she put the certificate in a sealed envelope with instructions that Shirley give it directly to her teacher and return it to her that same day. Shirley gave the envelope to her teacher and was stunned a short time later to be called to the office! Never one to cause trouble, she could not begin to imagine what the summons might mean. Imagine her surprise when the principal advised her they 'had a problem'! It seems there was a discrepancy as to her name! Her name? What?! At this point she was shown her birth certificate which stated, to her shock, her name was Shirley *Irene* not Shirley May as she had always been told. She was then informed that her mother would have to come in and straighten the matter out! All the rest of the day Shirley was tormented as to how she could possibly explain to her mother that she had to come to school the next day. Slowly, as the day progressed she began to realize that maybe the birth certificate was correct, as the principal had insisted! Now, after all, she hadn't even known her own name? How could that be?! She remembered the friend who had discovered, by accident, that she had been adopted. She told Shirley how she felt so terrible, as though she had lived a lie all her life. Shirley began to understand how she felt! That afternoon when she informed her mother of the problem her mother became livid! Red-faced, she angrily ordered Shirley into her room where she was to stay until her father returned home. Shaken more than ever, Shirley, of course, did as she was told. She always did. When her father came home her door remained shut until she was called for supper. After eating, as they did the dishes, her mother informed her she would accompany her to school the next morning. She did, and no more was said with the family, however, Shirley was advised she would be referred to as Shirley Irene from then on. When she questioned her mother she was told: "Don't let it throw you—WE know what your real name is, and that's all that matters! Those school people know nothing!" It wasn't until many years later, as an adult, she heard the actual story of how her God-Mother had passed on her own name to Shirley!

Before they moved from the Bungalow Shirley had pleaded with her father to hang a small gym-set from the porch ceiling, where she could use the trapeze and rings and do some acrobatics, while waiting for mothers' return to let her in. She really enjoyed this, having been able to learn some during the gym class. Next, she signed up at the local Park District which offered lessons in ballet, toe tap, acrobatics and tap dancing, all at no cost. Her parents were more than willing to let her do this and it was a great outlet for her, both physically and mentally. It allowed her to excel in something and possibly gain a little self esteem as well. Constantly being told one is stupid, incapable, can be a tough burden to bear. The plus was, that it was halfway between her school and home, so she was able to walk home in plenty of time to set the table. Then, after some time, an exhibition was held with all the young participants able to show off their talents. Parents were invited as well as the public. Classes were put into categories, according to age, and after much urging her parents agreed to attend. That night went quickly for her and the others as they alternately performed in the varied groups. Because Shirley had enrolled in all the classes, she was in each of them, but her highlight that evening was when the three top girls in acrobatics would do their special finale. The three stood next to thick ropes which were attached to the field house ceiling, quite a height! Soon the music began, their cue to begin climbing the ropes, with Shirley in the center and one girl on either side. Then, adding to the drama, the building was darkened with low lighting, but at the same time, bright spotlights shone on each of the young performers. Shirley led the others in their routine, which included somersaults, and hanging from strops by the ankles, up to the ending with something called a 'bird's nest'. She felt a real thrill as the cheers reached up to their ears. Then, it was over. They clambered down the ropes as the instructors took their bows to the audience appreciative applause. The three then took their bows together, beaming with accomplishment. It was time to seek out parents and head for home. Everett and Rose were not happy parents, to say the least. Rather than getting the praise she expected, she was removed from the classes and the inside gym set was gone the next day! No explanation was really given, she was simply told that they would not allow her to be killed by some insensitive strangers, and from here on she was to act like a lady, not some circus animal! So much for self-esteem!

When summer vacation came Shirley was able to find a job at a nearby grocery warehouse, typing up address labels. She made 25 cents an hour, and she loved the sense of freedom to work among people who, though older than she, were respectful of the way she did her job. For the first time in her life, outside of school, someone was complimenting her, telling her she was doing a fine job. She had come close to believing all the negative things she was constantly subjected to at home, but here were people treating her not only kindly but friendly.

On receiving her first paycheck, after two weeks work, she was so proud she nearly strutted home, anxious to show off. Looking at the amount of the check her mother informed her that $10.00 a week would be considered enough for room and board for now, until she finished school. Stunned, Shirley sputtered how she had hoped to buy some new clothes but she was interrupted by: "This is my house, and you will do as I say!" A phrase she would come to know quite well, along with her fathers: "Do as your mother says", they were like repeated mantras. Later, as the next few years flowed by, they added yet one more: "If you don't like things around her, there's the door."

As a result of such events, Shirley became withdrawn, living her life in the most routine way. She was ever fearful of making waves. While the move to living upstairs of a tavern had made life pleasurable for her parents, it added a new aspect to her life as well. She was allowed "to go out" after supper, to come in when the street lights came on. First time she walked out of the downstairs door she was surprised to see many young people right outside the doorway. Between the apartment building and the street there was a couple of feet of grass, and around that grass was an iron railing about two and a half feet high. There, perched on that railing were several boys and girls about her age, with legs swinging, they were laughing and talking, but when she appeared, all the talk stopped! Standing still, her hand still on the doorknob, she held her breath, not knowing what to do or say. Suddenly one of the young boys came toward her and said, "Hi, I'm Jack, welcome to the neighborhood!" Then they all came over and she found herself surrounded by smiling faces. Welcoming, smiling, faces! She soon discovered that the neighborhood they had moved into, was made up of families who had lived there for generations past. Because they all seemed to know one another so well, it was rather intimidating, but the amazing thing was, they all seemed anxious to put her at ease. The fact that she'd been put down so long, she simply assumed no one would want to be her friend, after all, what did she have to offer?! That year became her beginning of a real childhood! She came to know what a 'city kid' did for fun. These boys and girls all played happily together, out on Tripp Avenue. They were called the Tripp Avenue Gang (before the word 'gang' had the connotations it came to have), and joy of joy, she became a part of it all! There were games of red light-green light, kick the can, and as it began to get dark, there were games of hide and seek with the shouts of "Ollie Ollie Ocean Free" ringing up and down the block! During the warm days there were ongoing games of Monopoly that lasted for days, with the board set up on one or another's front porch. There was such open camaraderie. Such good, clean fun, spur of the moment games, were nothing like the structured games led by teachers at school. This was pure enjoyment of life. They made her feel a part of something, a feeling she'd never had before. She had never really felt like part of a family. Family? She thought to herself, that though she had a mother and a father, they didn't exist as a family unit, it was them against her. First it was Everett who had been on the outside, now, it seemed she was moved into that vacated spot!

On weekends and during summer vacation when the ice truck drove up under her apartment windows, and Tony the big, burly looking iceman came to deliver ice to the tavern, they would all wait around until he finished chipping at the huge blocks of ice. Then, with huge black, iron tongs, he would hoist these large blocks onto his shoulder which was covered with a padded affair that made him look like a catcher behind home plate. Soon as he entered the tavern door, the kid's would swarm to the back of the truck and grab one or two pieces of the ice. Then, sitting on porch steps they would enjoy what they considered a real treat, and what a treat it was, on a hot summer day in the city. They would tell of the different adventures they had at Nixon where they attended school, and Shirley, the only one who went to Barry, told them hers. She told them about the School Store across the street where a small group had lunch together. If they had an extra couple of pennies they could purchase an ice cream cone, where a small slip of paper in the bottom of the cone would sometimes inform them they had won a free cone. The ice cream bars, also carried a message, once licked clean there would sometimes appear the magic words "free bar", what a thrill to be a winner. Then there was the huge assortment of penny candies . . . tootsie rolls, dot's on a roll of paper, Mary Jane's, green spearmint leaves, malted milk balls, so many great things for a penny. She also told them of how the kid's would trade lunches oftentimes. Shirley's mother made the strangest sandwiches of all, at times, when they were out of baloney or spiced ham she would find a sliced cucumber or slice radish sandwich! The others thoughts that was fascinating so eagerly traded for their ham sandwiches and Shirley was equally thrilled. Then once lunch was done they would walk around the back of the school store, into the alleyway which was behind the Borden Milk Dairy. There, for all to see, and pet, were the horses who pulled the delivery trucks early in the morning. They came to know each horse and it's name, and of course developed favorites. Then, the winter before, during a severe cold spell Shirley and her friend were walking to school, trying to walk on the grass which wasn't nearly as slippery as the sidewalks. Suddenly, they heard a terrible sound. It was a huge thump, followed by the sound of breaking glass, accompanied by a high piercing scream! Shocked, they stood there, staring at the overturned milk truck and one of their horse friends skidding across the street! His four legs were up in the air, then he twisted and turned in pain, and they realized the screeching sounds were coming from the animals throat! Shortly after, the police cars arrived and the officers pushed Shirley and the other children who had been drawn to the scene, toward school. Big, friendly, Officer Tom came to meet them, and to help them cross Diversey Parkway to get to Barry School, which he did everyday, but this day was not the same. Shirley and the other children were stunned at seeing such a sight. It was even more devastating to learn the next day that the horse had been shot, right there on the street, where he lay screaming in pain.

Although they were reassured the horse was relieved of pain, none could reconcile themselves to ever pay visits to the horse barn after that sad day. The only time they ever ventured in the alleyway after that, was when the tar men came. They were a group of men who worked out of a large truck that towed behind it a vat of steaming tar! The tar was spread across the different roof tops, and the youngsters, loved watching and even the smell of the hot tar was good to their noses. They would begin to wheedle the working men to give each of them a small wad of the cooling tar, after which they would pop it into their mouths and chew with a passion! They always tried to convince each other that the tar was really good for their teeth, where they got that idea, who knows? Still they all managed to chew the black stuff as long as possible before spitting it out, onto the gravel playground!

This was an exciting time for Shirley, and a period of growth in many ways. During that summer, nearby Kelvyn Park High School opened it's indoor pool for kids in the neighborhood, and her new friends invited her to join them one day. That night, she got her mothers' reluctant permission, "so long as it doesn't cost anything", but she reminded Shirley she had no swimsuit. Shirley hastened to explain that one of her new friends had offered her an out-grown suit, having three sisters in one household they had many. She hardly slept that night, she was so excited.

Next day as they all walked together, one of her new friends, Dorothy, smiled happily at her, when her older sister, Ruth stopped suddenly and pointed at Shirley. "Hey!" she said, "You do know how to swim don't you?" Of course, she wasn't about to be left out at that point, after being invited, and having a suit! So she smiled and lied her assurance. How tough could it be, she thought, having been to Lake Michigan, as well as in Fox Lake where she had crawled along the beaches, she had no idea a pool could be much different. After the merry group showered and changed into their suits all five girls headed for the pool. Shirley was astonished as they emerged through the door, it was so noisy! Voices seemed to echo and resound off the walls! Then her eyes took in the size of the enormous pool. Frightened, still with Ruth in the lead, she followed along as they walked in single file to the edge, where one by one, each jumped in. Shirley had no idea what all the painted numbers on the side meant, certainly never occurred to her they told the depth of the water! Her head filled with the warm air and chlorine vapors, she never realized she might not be able to touch bottom! So when it came to her turn, she simply jumped!

Years later she never could remember exactly what happened. They told her she'd gone down and come up twice before they realized she wasn't playing around! Ruth jumped in beside her, keeping her head above water when she surfaced the third time. Scared? She was near hysterical, but more frightened of losing her newfound friends through her foolish lying, then the fact she had nearly drowned.

Ruth walked her to the ladder, then told the others to go on and play. She sat on the pool edge, her arm around Shirley's shoulder. She told her in no uncertain terms, how foolish she had been, and what could have-nearly did-happen! Head down, trying not to give way to tears and further embarrass herself, she nodded at Ruth's words. Ashamed, feeling foolish she sat, sure that Ruth would get up and leave her forever, but Ruth stood up and looking down, extended her hand and said: "Let's go girl, you have some lessons to learn. It's going to be a long hot summer and we have a lot of swimming days ahead." She never made Shirley feel like the freak she felt herself to be. None of the girls ever ridiculed her for her lack of knowledge about anything, and through them she learned about life from a city-kid's point of view. The bungalow's fenced in yard had kept her more isolated than she knew, but now she was living in a real Chicago neighborhood setting and it was her chance to learn many things. One thing she learned-quickly-was how to swim! In years to come she took Red Cross swimming classes, as well as lifeguard training. She loved the water and in her teens would spend many hours swimming 'off the rocks' at North Avenue Beach in Lake Michigan. In the future she would teach her children to swim and even rescued more than one youngster who had followed her foolish path.

Another thing that occurred that fall, was Shirley was invited to her first Halloween Party! Not just in a classroom, but at the home next door to her apartment building. The boy, Jerry, had it in his decorated basement. The entire neighborhood was invited, there was plenty of food as well as games to play. Shirley suddenly found herself over her head once again, but this time it wasn't in water. She was initiated into a game of Spin The Bottle. With all the boys and girls seated in a large circle, one would take a turn in spinning the milk bottle and whomever it pointed to, they would go off into the coal shed and kiss. (I realize how tame this sounds now, but she had never, ever been kissed by a boy and the very thought was scary.) When her turn came she was petrified. This boy, Jack, with whom she'd played kick the can, red rover, was hardly a frightening vision himself. Still . . . well, he gently leaned toward her, and even more gently touched his lips to hers and electricity flowed through her with a shock. Quickly, guilt filled, she pulled away. Everyone laughed as they emerged from the coal shed, but she found nothing to laugh at! When she returned home, at the designated time, Rose went into her room to ask what they had done at the party, and Shirley looked up at her mother . . . and burst into tears. Rose began to shake her, demanding to tell what she had done now. What stupid thing had she done? Finally, with tears running down her cheeks she confessed, she had sinned and thought she might be pregnant! (Imagine the shock Rose must have felt!) However, after much questioning and more shaking of shoulders, she discovered that her daughters' big sin was actually one innocent kiss. Sighing in relief, Rose told her to go to sleep, that her father was waiting for her to go downstairs with him, but they would "have a talk in the morning." As she was leaving Rose turned around, learned over Shirley, and said in an almost compassionate voice: "Believe me, you are NOT pregnant." Although her mother's words had obviously been meant to allay her fears, she lay wide-eyed awake for a long time before sleep claimed her. As fearful as she had been of having a baby she was nearly as frightened of 'the talk' they were to have in the morning. But, talk they did. Although by modern standards it was not the best of mother-daughter talks, bordering on the birds and bees theme, it was enough to allow Shirley to realize she'd done nothing terrible, after all. What it did do, however, was cause her to seek more information, because here was yet another area of ignorance she needed to clear up. The only source of knowledge she was familiar with was the library, and she had no idea how to search for answers there. But her further education on the subject would come sooner than she knew then.

One evening there came a knock on the apartment door, which was off the kitchen. Everett sat in the parlor in his chair, where he read the paper and listened to the radio on their radio/record player. Meanwhile, as usual, Rose sat at one end of the kitchen table, reading the rest of the paper, while Shirley sat at the other end doing her homework. Shirley was only allowed in the parlor on Sunday mornings when she could look at the funnies after returning from church, other than that she was to stay in the kitchen or in her own room. Rose opened the door at the knock, and stepped back in surprise, then sarcastically announced: "Well, look who is here!" Shirley sat staring, overwhelmed to see her big brother standing there in uniform, so handsome and grown up! As she started to get up her father came storming out into the kitchen and without blinking an eye said: "What the hell are YOU doing here?" Unable to believe her ears Shirley just gaped. Then her brother turned to her, with his old cocky grin and said: "Well, sis, how are YOU?" She stammered how she was fine and so glad to see him . . . but her fathers' voice cut across her words as he ordered Everett to "Get out-once and for all-get out!" As he turned to leave he looked over his shoulder at her and said: 'I'll write you, Shirl, write back, okay?" And he was gone. No homework was completed that night, instead Shirley went to her room and mulled over what changes had come over Everett. HER brother was in the Army Air Corp! Her own brother! How exciting was that?! She wondered how it had all come to be. It would be sometime before she discovered he had been in the ROTC program, and become interested in flying. It was through this connection he had enlisted at the age of 17 and was now in the Service. It was 1941.

In 1941 Shirley was a 13 year old who had so little knowledge about the world and what was going on in it! There was talk of war, but she had no real idea of what that could mean nor foresee it having any impact on her or her life. She was a typical self-centered young girl. Her thoughts consisted of the fact she would graduate in June of 1942 and would be a student at Kelvyn Park High School in the fall. She'd been a fairly good student but geography and history were most boring to her. She had loved English, simply because throughout her childhood, having no playmates, her books were her friends. In reading she had read of other countries and cultures, yet when Pearl Harbor was bombed, it seemed so very far away. Hawaii? Some island in the Pacific was all she could recall. Suddenly though, she was forced to grow up in a very shocking way. The older brothers of her friends were enlisting, and going off to war. Her next door neighbor, who had hosted her first Halloween Party a short time before, enlisted shortly after she began her Freshman year. The fellow students she had come to know as juniors or seniors were all leaving school, enlisting, and going off to war. The brother of a brother-sister cheerleading team at Kelvyn enlisted. Then, as Shirley began her second year of high school she was forced to accept the closeness of World War II, it was no longer some far away happening. At the movie theatres there was always a Pathe News Report which featured many of the servicemen and updates of the war. Because this was pre-television days, these were shocking pictures for all to view. The selling of War Bonds was carried on all around. Shirley saved the .25¢ war stamps in a special paper book, which when filled would cover the price of an $18.75 War Bond, but worth $25.00 when redeemed at a future date. She and her fellow students held fundraisers to help in the war effort. Everyone saved the foil from cigarette packages, from gum, and then rolled them into huge balls to be donated along with metal pots and pans, all to go to the making of war weapons. There were many celebrities who made personal appearances throughout the states, all to raise awareness of the war effort. Shirley got to see James Cagney one day, just blocks from home. She began to listen to the radio news reports, which she had never done before. She went to school one morning to find that the brother half of the cheerleading team had been killed. Students mourned the loss of one of their own. Then not much after, her friend, Jerry, was shipped home in a closed casket. He had become infected with an infectious disease. All the neighborhood attended the wake, and wept. One of the boys Shirley had been to the movies with, a few times, who had gifted her with his framed graduation picture the year before, followed soon after. He, too, was returned in a closed casket having blown most of the side of his head off through a bazooka that misfired! Within months that year, dozens of schoolmates had been injured or killed. It was time to face and accept reality, and it wasn't easy for Shirley. Her constant fear of where Everett was, and if he was alright was made even more difficult because she couldn't share those feelings with her parents. Off and on she had received mail from him, but since the war, many were censored. Sentences were cut out to an extent that they barely made any sense. It was a frightening time for many. Yet the young men kept volunteering because Uncle Sam needed them and they were more than willing to fight the enemy. Germany had joined with Japan and Hitler and Tojo were the most hated people of the time. Even cartoons at the movies highlighted the hatred and when the USA was shown the winner of a conflict the cheering could be heard out on the street. Just as when they were young and booed the bad guy in the many Western movies, the youth now booed their country's enemies. Everyone gathered around their radio to hear F.D.R. give his historical 'Fireside Chats'. Politics didn't matter then, everyone depended on their President to lead them to the winning of this conflict. Everyone trusted Franklin Delano Roosevelt, division wasn't possible, we are "all in this together—to defeat the enemy."

Meanwhile Shirley was feeling a bit more self-assured in high school than grade school, yet there was still a trace of intimidation, especially due to her height (or lack of it). She was slightly over 4'11" and shorter than most of her classmates. Standing in the lunchroom line there was always someone who would ask how the weather was "down there", or worse yet, get in front of her and say: "Shorty won't mind . . ." Thanks to her parents continued reinforcement of her stupidity it never crossed her mind to stand up for herself. She let it go, but inner resentment built up over the years.

Back on her first day of high school she had slowly made her way to the huge study hall set up for incoming freshmen, when she looked up at a sea of faces as unsure as her own and her eyes locked with a girl who was familiar. Making her way toward her, thinking what fantastic luck this was, she realized the girl was someone she knew from Barry grade school Although they had never been fast friends they did know one another. In 8th grade they were seated by alphabetical order, and Shirley's last name started with "V" and this girl, Doris, had a last name that started with "T" so they were seatmates of a sort. Doris spent the entire 8th grade seated behind her! Still, it was a friendly face and she must have felt the same way, because she worked her way toward Shirley as well. Soon they were seated together, sitting through orientation and comparing classes, finding several together. Having one another helped both to feel braver to face the days ahead as lowly freshies! Time passed, new acquaintances were made but Doris and Shirley remained close friends. Then one day Doris invited Shirley to come to her house after school, of course she had to say no, because she would first need permission from her mother, she explained. But, shyly she added, she'd ask about the next day, if that would be okay. Doris said that would be great. Shirley found it difficult to believe she could just invite someone to her home without first getting permission from her parents. Shirley had never had a friend just 'come over' not even the neighborhood kids who had become her friends over the past summer. They, on the other hand, would often have Shirley in to play a game when it was too hot to be on their porches. It never entered her mind to have them come up to the apartment where she lived. They all lived in big, old houses, she, in the small, cramped apartment. Besides where would they sit? There were only four chairs in the kitchen, and certainly nothing but standing room in her bedroom, unless they were to perch on her bed (which wasn't allowed, anyway!). When she got home that day, after leaving Doris, she began to dwell on the differences of her life and the ones her friends all seemed to live. She sat on the hallway steps, waiting for her mother to come home and let her in, and the longer she sat the more she began to realize what a strange situation she was in. She had two parents, her own bedroom, but she never seemed to feel she had a 'home'. The apartment where they slept and had their meals was just that: a place to sleep and eat. Even at mealtimes, she realized, she often felt an intruder, of sorts. She was not allowed to take part in the conversations between her parents. She was advised to eat—not talk. It often felt a sort of 'them' and 'me' thing, yet she had never really recognized it until then. She wondered if maybe Doris was the strange one, and her parents the unique ones, and determined to find out.

When Rose arrived home, they entered the apartment and Shirley asked if it would be possible for her to go straight to her friend, Doris' home after school the next day so they could study together. It was quiet for a few minutes, and she held her breath, waiting. Then her mother turned and looked at her with narrowed eyes, and asked why they should have to study together? Was she that dumb, in such dire need, that she had to get help from a fellow-student? Didn't she have an ounce of pride?! Shirley patiently replied that they actually only had a couple of the same classes, if just seemed a 'fun' way to study, plus she added, quickly, she could probably get all her homework done before supper, by having a table to work on and not waiting on the hall steps. After some deliberation Rose relented, but demanded Shirley's promise to be home by 4 o'clock so she could get the table set for supper. Oh, and did Shirley promise!

The next day brought a real turning point in Shirley's life, but she didn't know it then. She and Doris walked the few blocks to where Doris lived. She lived in a two-story apartment house, and as they neared it, she took out her key to let them in. Revelation number one—of many to come. She had her own key?! Was able to have access to the whole apartment and her parents weren't even there?

"Where are your folks?" Shirley asked. Doris explained that they were both at work and never minded if she brought friends home. As Shirley stood staring at her, Doris never noticed because she'd tossed her books on the couch and was heading for the kitchen. Over her shoulder she called to Shirley: "Why are you standing there—holding your books? Toss them next to mine! Ya wanna' Pepsi?" This last was said as she extended a bottle of Pepsi Cola toward her friend. Shirley had never had a whole 16-ounce bottle of pop in her life! Sometimes her mother would send her downstairs to buy a quart of root beer but that was a special treat, and she only had a glassful. That bottle of Pepsi was truly a "big deal" to Shirley, but she wasn't going to let Doris know, of course.

Soon they settled down at the dining room table. (Shirley couldn't help but think that the times she had been allowed at the dining room table had been few and far between. On Holidays or some special occasion.) As they did their homework they would look up now and then and talk some nonsense and it was so very wonderful. Shirley's first real friendship. She felt she was becoming part of a new world, to actually have a friend of her own, not one in a group. It had been great to be allowed to be a part of the neighborhood kid's on the block, but deep in her heart she knew this was something special. Most of those neighborhood teens had opted for a different high school so she saw them seldom now. As days grew into weeks and then months, Doris and Shirley became as close as sisters neither of them had. Doris was an only child, and in essence so was Shirley. They would share their innermost secrets and desires with each other. At last, there was someone to talk to about girl things.

The first time Doris asked Shirley to spend the night one Friday, she never thought she'd get permission, but to her surprise, her parents seemed pleased to know she was "keeping busy and staying out of trouble." (Years later, when Shirley became a parent she couldn't believe they had never tried to befriend Doris' parents to be assured she was in good company. They had never even called them to check if Shirley was welcome. Strange, especially considering how often she was told how foolish and stupid she was . . . didn't it even occur to them she might get into some serious trouble?)

Shirley thought she would always remember the Saturday afternoon she and Doris walked into their apartment to find her Dad lying on the couch with her mother stretched out next to him, spoon fashion, listening to the radio! She was actually so taken aback she couldn't believe what she was seeing. Soon as she and Doris reached Doris' bedroom Shirley asked why they were behaving like THAT?! "Like what?" she asked. "Lying together, out in the open, my gosh they look like something out of a movie!" Doris could not understand her obvious consternation, "Why, they do that all the time, whenever we listen to our nightly radio shows. They lay there on the couch and I usually lay on the floor in front of the radio. What is wrong with you? Don't your parents do the same stuff?" Shirley was sure her face would split from her effort to keep from laughing out loud! The very thought of her mother and father in such a compromising position almost did her in! (Children always fight the thought of their parents having sex, of course, but—) Still, the more she noticed the other activities in her friends home, the reaching out to one another they did, she knew at last, THIS was what a family was, what a home should be! The on-going showing of affection she found rather embarrassing at first, then before she even realized it, she found herself being included-in the hugs, the goodnight kisses. Surprise! Surprise! She found she enjoyed it.

Problem was, the comparison of the lack of affection in her own home life became more apparent than ever. She understood, at last, hers was the odd family not her friends, and it was not a happy discovery at all. But she did learn something then. She learned that showing affection to each other is a good thing, a nurturing thing, and something she would pass on to her children if the Lord allowed her to have any. The old doubts still lay under the surface, and she still felt inadequate at times. Would someone really ever marry her and give her the ideal family she dreamed of having? She and Doris often talked about their future, and she had shared her dream of having at least four children: two boys, two girls. Shirley had confessed to Doris how she had always thought that something was lacking in her. She told how she was treated, continually told how stupid she was. How she felt so useless when told she couldn't do anything right. How she was unable to take an active part in a family life, because they didn't have a family life. She even shared one of the many stories like the time she had put a kettle of water on the stove for a cup of tea. She had not wiped the kettle bottom, after filling it, and the drops of water made a hissing sound in the flame, the Rose was there in a shot! Reaching out to shut the stove knobs off, she angrily told Shirley to never use HER stove again. If she didn't have enough sense to dry a kettle she should stay away from her things!

A couple of years later though, when she was 16, she was granted permission to use that stove. She was instructed to fix supper for her father and herself while Rose was out shopping. There were no malls then, but she left by 10 a.m. and didn't return until about 6 p.m. She would be laden with shopping bags filled with dried apricots, pretzels, and other special things for the week ahead. She lugged these bags, taking three different streetcars each way. Shirley and her father would eat their lonely meal, with little or no conversation, after which he would retire to the parlor while she stayed in the kitchen.

One of those Saturday evenings after she had fixed supper for her father and herself she was finishing the dishes when the current roomer came into the kitchen. He sat at the table and when she finished up, she joined him. He was a pleasant enough individual who pretty much kept to himself. They carried on a light conversation, which eventually turned to the topic of the war. The war had cast a cloud over everyone, and as they spoke of the latest news, he asked her if she thought her brother might be in active combat. She was surprised to learn he even knew she had a brother, but responded with sadness, that she was rather sure that was the case, due to the lack of letters. Next day she repeated the conversation and was told by her mother, in no uncertain terms, she was to have no family discussion with this man or anyone else, especially since she insisted on referring to Everett as "my brother!"

Living right on Fullerton Avenue, which was a streetcar line, made it possible to use that wonderful mode of transportation which stopped right on their corner. Streetcar fare was three cents which got you a transfer to continue on as many cars as it took to get to your destination, with just a punch on that paper transfer. Shirley's father had never had a vehicle that she remembered, but once when questioned he became very upset stating one was not needed with the streetcar so near. Later, her mother told her that he had driven at one time, but a young boy on a bicycle had run into him, going through his windshield! Although it had not been his fault, and no one was seriously injured, her father chose never to drive again.

At times Doris would come over to Shirley's and join in with the "gang" from Tripp Ave. and ride with Jerry in his beat up old Ford, to Russell's Bar B Que. It was during this time that Doris met one of the Tripp gang whom everyone called "Red", due to his mop of red hair. Any dating they did, Shirley would go with one of the boy's and Doris would team up with Red. Shirley had no serious intentions and assumed Doris didn't either, but . . . time would prove otherwise.

That year they both got jobs at a nearby solder factory, located between each of their homes, about a four block walk for each, in opposite directions. At first they worked after school and weekends, but as summer approached and school vacation was due they planned on how it would be if they could work the nightshift. (From 4 to 12 midnight) It would not only mean a nickel an hour more, but would fit into their more farfetched plans! Gaining permission wasn't nearly as difficult as Shirley thought it might be, because her mother realized that the fulltime pay Shirley would earn would mean more income for her as well. Besides, she was told, it would keep her "out of trouble", which Shirley had a hard time understanding, never having gotten into trouble! During those days, in the '40's it was not a fearful thing for young girls to walk even after midnight. Their plan was to get up early, same as on a school day, meet in front of the factory where they worked and then walked several blocks to the end of the bus line. At Crawford Ave. (which was later named Pulaski Rd.) they would board the bus which would take them straight to North Avenue beach, and 'the rocks'. They always got choice seats and for five cents were transported to another world. They wore their swimsuits under their clothing, and on arrival would strip off their clothes and sunbathe on towels. No one ever heard of sun damage or cancer causing rays their only concern was to get a great tan and not a sunburn. They'd use a combination of baby oil and iodine, or just cocoa butter.

When it got too warm they would dive into the cool waters of beautiful Lake Michigan. There was no beach, no sand, just the massive rocks where they could dive into the water. What a glorious summer that was. The sun, the water and great looking lifeguards to flirt with, what more could two young girls ask for on summer vacation? They got it down to a science as to exactly how long they had before they would tear off for the bus to take them home. Walking from the bus line back to the factory, on to their own homes, only to change clothes and meet back at the factory to work 4 to midnight! Tired? No, not when you are a 16-year-old girl just tasting the reality of freedom. A memorable summer, indeed, and they hated to see it come to an end. But, of course, as all good things do, end it did.

The two friends continued to reach out and make many more acquaintances, yet were always there for one another. It was still a time of sharing ideas and dreams and it was a freeing time for Shirley especially, knowing she could be herself and not be criticized. They met another young woman whose name was Grace and the three of them formed a circle of friendship. The three would often go on long bike rides on weekends. School life was much easier once that freshman year had been completed.

The two girls hoarded their summer money and were looking forward to shopping for skirts, sweaters, bobby six and penny loafers (the teen 'uniform' of the day). As the weekend approached Shirley mentioned to her mother that she and Doris were going to shop at Logan Square, which they could walk to. Rose turned a shocked face to her and said: "For what? What would you need to shop for, you can still wear the clothes you have, and besides I have no extra money for you." So, smiling her sweetest smile, Shirley informed her that she had been saving from her summer job and should have enough to get a few things. There followed one of those 'loud silences' one hears of, then Rose sputtered: "Just how much money did you save?" She knew Shirley had given her the regular $10.00 a week so couldn't imagine it would be a large sum. Feeling so proud of herself, so anxious to prove she was not as stupid as she'd been told, she didn't have sense enough to hesitate. Instead she blurted out how she had been given a 5 cent an hour raise for working midnights, plus she had been working 40 hour weeks, spending only bus fare all that time. (There was actually no time to spend money.) Foolish girl-she was so proud. She actually took a step backward as she saw her mother smile that silky smile she had, as she informed Shirley if she was old enough to work she was old enough to pay board! "Board?", Shirley gasped, unbelieving, BOARD?! I am not one of your boarders, I'm your daughter!" Rose, her arms across her chest, simply said, "We'll see, after I've talked to your father you'll see." That evening they must have talked all right, because as she was leaving for school Shirley was informed she would pay $15, a week from now on. After all, there was not only the board, but her laundry was done for her as well as her meals prepared, what could she expect? The $10. She'd paid the summer before had only lasted as long as she worked, but now that she would continue to work as well as go to school it was time for her to face up to her responsibilities. Time to grow up! That evening when her father came home from work she approached him to see if this was really true—and again was told: "You do as your mother says." "But" Shirley started to say, only was cut off with: "That'll do young lady, I'll hear no more about it." Up went the newspaper, in front of his face, his barrier from any further conversation. Crestfallen, Shirley went to her room to wonder how she had been foolish enough to get herself in this mess. Next morning, when she shared the news with Doris, her friend simply couldn't understand. How could she? Shirley couldn't understand herself! Still, now and again when the opportunity arose she would put in any extra time she could and pocket the money. She quickly figured out that the best (and only) method was to have her check cashed before going home, hand her mother the $15. And squirrel away the rest . . . for a sweater or skirt, whatever. Surprisingly, Rose never asked to see check stubs.

Yet another summer approached once again, but Doris was dating only "Red", and the two girls saw less and less of each other. Mostly, Shirley dated guys who were seniors or already out of school, feeling those in her own class were juvenile acting. This was brought to light especially after her body had undergone drastic changes over the past summer. When she entered high school she still wore undershirts under her clothing, no such thing as 'training bras' in those days! But suddenly it seemed, as summer wore on she felt in need of support and finally mentioned it to her mother. Her mother checked her out and agreed she should have a bra. That Saturday they went to Lincoln, Belmont and Ashland Avenues where Rose went each week, and they walked from store to store. Shirley had been to Logan Square, but this much larger area was amazing to her, who had never seen such a stretch of block after block of places to explore. All down the streets, store after store, clothes, furniture, meat, shoes, it was a revelation. To Roses' credit she took her young daughter to a department store where she could be fitted properly. Imagine Shirley's pride, as she left wearing a size 34B! However on returning to school that fall she lost that feeling of pride in a hurry. The boys were disgusting to her eyes.

They ogled—leered, and made snide comments as she walked by. She soon found it to her advantage to wear larger sized sweaters. She even found the girls' reactions to be obscene as well! Some actually accused her of stuffing her bra with tissues (as many of them did), but in the locker room where they were forced to disrobe and shower before swimming class they quickly found out the truth!

The more Doris became involved with Red, the less time she and Shirley spent together, of course. At first it was hard for Shirley to not feel jealous, left out. Yet she cared so much for her friend she could only be happy for her. Their friendship continued, with telephone calls at night and hurried conversations in school. Eventually Shirley made several other friends and although she knew she would never be as close to another female as she had been with Doris, life was still good.

That summer Shirley was asked by her boss at the factory if she would be interested in working there during the summer once again, but days, and in the main office. Well, of course she was flattered, and thinking that she would, in time be making her living in one office or another, this practical experience could be a gift. She accepted. Her father had 'set her straight' on the possibility of attending college. He simply stated that unless she wished to be a nurse or a teacher there was no reason for her to go beyond high school. He felt he was a good example, being a tool and dye maker, earning good wages, and he'd only completed the 4th grade. He advised her to get any such 'high and mighty' ideas out of her head! So, at the age of 17 she began what she thought to be the beginning of her life's career.

One day one of the women who worked in the office approached Shirley to see if she knew her son, seems he'd graduated two years before from Kelvyn Park High School. While Shirley thought he seemed vaguely familiar she didn't feel she really knew him and said as much to Gladys. The next day Gladys brought in a framed picture of him, in his Air Corps (now known as the Air Force) uniform. What a hunk! He was quite attractive, and the uniform added to it. Because the young men she and Doris had worked on the nightshift with the summer before had all enlisted in the service, she had begun writing letters to each of them. Then she was asked to write to others, and soon was writing to all the servicemen from the factory, in addition to those from the neighborhood. It became quite a task, in the days before computers, or even electric typewriters, still it made her feel she was doing something toward the war effort. Keeping up the morale of those so far from home, and they responded eagerly, enclosing snapshots which she could share with those who knew them. Shirley suggested to Gladys she give her the address and she would include him in her letter writing campaign. Her son was already on his way back home, she was told, but she'd make sure they met, because she felt Shirley was a nice girl her "Buddy" would enjoy knowing. Shirley thought no more about it.

Shortly after that, as Shirley came out of the office, there was this beautiful big Oldsmobile with a couple of young guys in it, driving by. As they noticed her they began yelling silly things out the windows like: "Hi beautiful, would you like a ride?", "You sure look lonely", etc. Shirley just laughed at them and continued walking home. It was quite a boost to this young 17 year olds' ego as they continued to circle the couple blocks and catch up to her again and again. Finally, she neared Fullerton Avenue and they continued on their way. However, the next day, as she came out of the office door there was that Olds again! Because there was no other route she could take, she tried to ignore them as they continued to drive along side of her, calling to her. As she once more neared Fullerton Avenue, the car came to a stop and the driver jumped out and ran up to her. Standing before her, blocking her way, he asked if he had been alone would she have joined him? Accepted his ride offer? Shirley told him no, she said she had been brought up to go out with people to whom she had been properly introduced. With that having been said, she held her head high and walked across Fullerton Avenue and on up to the apartment. Still, climbing those stairs she had to smile to herself. The weekend had passed and having completed and always busy Monday, getting caught up with the paper work, Shirley slowly made her way out the office door, looking forward to relaxing, when to her surprise there was the Olds again! In her quick glance she took in the fact that the driver of the days' before was now in the passenger seat, quickly he jumped out and headed toward her as did his companion. As they headed Shirley's way she stood unsure of what to do or say. Smiling broadly he pleaded with her to please, just wait a minute. So she did, until they both stood before her. Yesterday's driver turned to his friend and said: "Okay, do it!" Whereupon his friend spoke up telling Shirley: "This is my friend Rick." He went on stating Rick's age, address, where he worked and added, almost breathlessly: "and he'd like to meet you." Shirley just stood there, gaping stupidly and he urged, "Please, uh, YOUR name is?" "Shirley." There upon he introduced them, in as polite a way as possible, and then turned and left to sit in the car. Of course, this broke Shirley up, and laughing she asked what was that all about, anyway? "Well", Rick explained, "you said you needed to be properly introduced and so I took care of it as best I knew how, so now, will you join me? I promise to drive careful, and get you right home safely, but I sure would like to get to know you." Not believing this was happening to her, she didn't know how to respond. (Sure, she thought, Doris has a steady guy who really seems to love her, many of the girls from school did, but what did she have of offer anyhow? Even her parents agreed that she was pretty much worthless, yet here was this nice looking young man seeking her out. Diligently seeking her out, in fact.) These thoughts literally flew through her mind as she tried to make a decision. She decided to see just how much he did want to get to know her as he professed, so she told him, she thought it would be nice to have his company—walking home with her. No car riding. So he happily joined her as his friend slowly tailed behind in the Olds. After a couple of days Shirley finally gave Rick her telephone number, and they became acquainted after many conversations, and eventually they dated. Although they never had a serious relationship, like marriage talks, he was the one to introduce her to sex. Her first. Like everything Rick did, he did it 'the right way'. No back seat quickie for him, oh no. He took her home to where she might meet his folks, then one day, after they left, he took her to his bed. He was a gentle, caring and wonderful lover. She was fortunate, she always thought, to have had him 'initiate' her, because she suffered no pain, nor did she feel guilt. Rick drove hotrods on a dirt track and Shirley would often go to watch him race. It was exciting, and seeing how respected and well liked he was by his many friends, she wasn't surprised to see how he was sought after by the many females present. Still, he always stayed close to her, protected her from any of the other drivers and made her feel safe. He also made her feel worthwhile for the first time in her life, he complimented her, and took her wherever he felt she would like to go. Then the relationship simply dissolved, for no particular reason. They simply went in different directions, maybe due to the fact he was considering becoming a pro racer, and she was facing yet another year of high school! Whatever, he was an important part of Shirley's growing up and needed to be mentioned here.

Problem was, after Rick had shown her the joy of sex, she sought out those who she sensed could satisfy her need to be wanted—without being used. Mostly she dated college guys or returning servicemen she'd written to, anyone with a couple years of living past her age. Soon she found herself drinking alcohol, and in general 'very grown up'—no wonder the 'kids' at school were such a bore to her. No more Sock-Hops for this gal, no weekends at the Aragon, Dutch Mill, etc. were much nicer she thought.

In her Senior year of high school Shirley got a job in the student councilors' office and was able to put out feelers in the area to find a job she could consider for after graduation. Working in the office of the factory had been a good introduction to the working world, but she felt she could do better. Doris, on the other hand, was planning a completely different move! She sought permission from the school authorities, and was granted it, to be married in March. They would graduate in June and she would turn 18 in August, what was the hurry Shirley wondered? While she now knew the joy of the opposite sex, and all that could involve, she could not imagine settling down for sometime. Although the girls continued to speak often, their relationship was on a different plane, Doris now had Lee to confide in. Shirley, felt no need to confide in anyone, she felt she was riding the crest of her youth and enjoying every minute of it.

Going to local bars, drinking alcohol with dates seemed rather natural to her, after all, her parents enjoyed the activity why then shouldn't she? Looking back, years later, she thought it a miracle she had not gotten into serious trouble during those months, or worse yet, become an alcoholic! She continued to date regularly on Friday night and weekends, but was discriminate as to who she dated and always 'policed' her own behavior in a cautious way. It seemed a wonder to her to have her

Sunday afternoons free, and not be dragged along to taverns as she had been as a little girl. During the Depression many lost their jobs, as did her father, when his plant shut down. He became active in politics and working for the city as a 'liquor inspector' was part of his job. Sunday after Sunday the three would go from tavern to tavern, while her parents sat at the bar and he 'conducted his business' with Shirley sitting in a nearby booth. Drinking soda and eating the popcorn and pretzels available to patrons at no cost soon became a staple in her life! She didn't mind too much, except when old, half drunken men, with their breath smelling like hounds from hell, would come over to her and give her nickels, sometimes dimes, for being such a 'little sweety'. She dared not complain to her parents, so she suffered silently and quickly learned to hide these gifts, rather than put them in the jukebox! Soon as they returned home she would sock away those coins, bringing them to school the next day, and hiding them in her desk, where she might buy something special at the school store where, as mentioned before, many things could be purchased for pennies at a time.

While she had enjoyed working in the office at the Solder factory, she discovered through her work for the Guidance Counselor, at Kelvyn Park, a job she felt sounded quite interesting. She applied for it, and succeeded in getting it. She was able to work weekends, and through the high school senior program, would put in two hours a day during the week. Ironically, it was right down the street from Doris but she seldom saw her as she left school early to get to work. She began with doing the normal type of office work she had done before, typing, filing, whatever she was called on to do. But one day, her boss asked her to come in on Saturday to learn a new job. That morning he explained to her what he wanted to do. He had a new, he thought, innovated idea he wanted to try. In his position he would meet with representatives from other companies who wished to purchase the many parts we made. He said it was often difficult to get an overall view as to inventory, plus it was time-consuming checking with each department. His idea was for Shirley to create charts, graph-like, which would give a clear picture as to what was immediately ready for purchase. It seemed that Shirley's referrals along with her resume had mentioned her artistic abilities and he thought she would be perfect for the job! She was thrilled at the idea, even though she would no longer have her own desk (which she'd treasured), she would be ensconced in a special area, with a large drawing table to work on. She would have all the colored pencils, post-board she requested, and had a month to come up with the finished product he could show to the Company Board of Directors.

As it turned out, she loved what she was doing and within only a couple weeks she had enough done for him to make his presentation. It was widely accepted and he and Shirley became known as Production Control! What a coup! She received a raise in pay, besides the bonus granted her, and she knew she had found a niche where she really belonged.

Her social life picked up as well, one of the bookkeeper's would spend time with her whenever he was near her department. He asked her to come watch the Company bowling team, of which he was a member, promising to drive her home afterward. She would walk the two blocks right from work, and enjoyed these times. Although he was nearly ten years her senior they became an item of sorts, and enjoyed each others company. Meantime, she continued dating others, and when her date would drop her off, she would stop "downstairs" in the tavern where her parents sat. She finally came to realize exactly what their ritual was all about. It consisted of her parents sitting on 'their' stools, drinking, her father playing dice games, and her mother dancing and flirting with the men. In general they seemed to be having a good time, and welcomed her to join them. Sitting on the next barstool she was encouraged to sip her mother's gin-buck, if she chose! Of course she chose! Wasn't she living the magic life?! She began to understand now, why when they would come upstairs after their 'ritual' they would be so loud and often arguing. One would think she, in turn, would have seen this as a reason not to drink. But no! She continued to go to taverns when on dates, taking great pride in the fact she never got drunk. The one thing she knew was how much she could drink and still be in complete control! She was probably a poor candidate for alcoholism simply because of her determination not to be like her mother! Yet, she was only a senior in high school and had tried about every drink available, even tried smoking, but didn't like the taste of cigarettes. So, although both her parents smoked she didn't. As for drugs! Never heard of them! Only in Charlie Chan movies when they spoke of opium dens, was she ever exposed to such knowledge. No, she just took part in the things she liked best: Her job, dating, which might include drinking and/or sex. She thought she had it made.

There was one fly in the ointment though, every time her parents got into an argument or were angry about something, the topic always seemed to turn to Shirley. How she was out running around doing who knew what. What did she do on these dates? Finally after being accused of wrong doing, she felt this was the perfect excuse she needed for doing what she knew was wrong. She rationalized that having the name she might as well play the game. Not a good decision, but it allowed her to justify her actions, which even she didn't approve of! Then there came the morning she awoke ill. So ill, she didn't think she could get out of bed, but she did. She went to work, as it was spring break from school and she was anxious to keep a good work record, expecting to spend many years in her new workplace. But Life turned out not to be as magic as she'd thought! As the day progressed she became her old self once again, and so assumed she'd just gotten a cold. Yet, next morning the sickness was back. She hung over the toilet bowl, retching, stomach heaving and thinking death would be welcome! Again she made it to work, but not so sure now, she didn't know after all, what was wrong. Checking her calendar, sure enough, she was late with her period. How late she didn't know, always have been irregular at best. That night she sat down and went back over the dates again and again. If she had been ill in the morning she was really in bad shape that night! Shirley knew without a doubt, all her 'fun-times' had caught up with her. She was pregnant. She found it hard to believe and even harder to accept, yet deep inside realized it was a fact, but what to do? She could not raise a child on her own, and knew as well, her parents would not help! Seventeen years old, with her "whole life ahead of her" she thought, at least that's what everyone was always saying. There was one young man whom she had dated, he was 22 when she met him, and in his last year of college. He was hoping to be a coach, dearly loved sports of all kinds. He had taken Shirley to many college football and basketball games, their dates had always been on a friendship level. He was like her older brother (the brother she continued to miss) he was always respectful and caring with her. She truly did not want to turn to him for help, he who had never more than lightly kissed her at the end of a date. She hated for him to know she had not acted so wisely with other dates. Yet he was the most responsible person she knew and trusted, so she got herself together, and told him of her situation. He was totally shocked, as she had expected, but he patted her shoulder and soothed away her tears, telling he would help, to just give him a few days. Two days later he called and told her he know of a 'trustworthy' doctor who would perform an abortion, although they were illegal, remember it was the 1940's! He assured Shirley he would not harm her physically. She tearfully thanked him and asked him to make whatever arrangements were needed. But he said no, he would not get involved any further, it would be up to her to make the call, get the money, whatever. Shirley didn't know it then, but she would never see nor hear from Lou again. She called the doctor, and using the 'correct wording' she'd been given, set up her appointment for the following week. She arranged for the surgery to be on a Friday, foolishly believing she would be back to work on Monday, with no more 'problem' and no one the wiser. She asked one of the girl's in the office to accompany her, telling her the truth, trusting her secrecy. Although they had never been close, the girl agreed. The doctor, was indeed, a doctor! He had an office and a nurse who assisted. They explained the procedure, advising her to stay quiet for the next couple days, as there would be bleeding. Afterward, driven home by her friend, she went to bed feigning sudden illness. Because it was a Friday her mother was home doing the weekly housecleaning. Her mother was not overly concerned, though Shirley was seldom ill, she just assumed it was a summer cold. Crawling into bed, Shirley refused dinner due to stomach cramps and a fever, and it was accepted. She took the pills the doctor had given her and spent most of the weekend in bed. When her mother realized she was having her period she simply chalked up the illness to being "that time of the month". Shirley did return to work after a few days, and though she was pale and drawn looking it was to be expected, everyone having been told of her "terrible cold." Now, however, it can be realized how fortunate she was to have been led to a real doctor, in sterile conditions. She could have been turned over to a butcher and paid for her sins for the rest of her life! Or quite possibly, with her life itself, as many others did in those days. There was no such thing as birth control pills then, and many a desperate girl died horribly. Shirley realized that for all her feelings of being an adult—when it came right down to facts, she had been acing like a näive child, not to mention stupid! It seemed to her that her parents were right after all, she was stupid!

During the days to come she spent many hours mulling over how she had nearly ruined her life forever. She really grew up then and began to act like the adult she had formerly thought herself to be. Dating no longer seemed to be anything she wanted to do. There were no more taverns in her life! She concentrated on her schoolwork and her job, and doing both as well as she could. Shirley found herself accepted by her fellow-workers, despite her youth, her position in Production Control helped in that area, but having self-esteem was the real answer. She took great pride in her job, and became friends with several of her co-workers. Although she sometimes went to watch the Company bowling team and her friend, Richard, drove her home, it was simply as friends they continued their relationship. It had never been much more than that, perhaps a goodnight kiss here and there, but Shirley discouraged even that light contact. The young woman who had accompanied her to the doctor had left as her family moved out of state, so there was no one to know of her indiscretion, and she realized it was up to her, and her alone, to mold a future for herself, and she set out to do just that!

Meanwhile, though, her home life had really deteriorated, worsening day by day. She had come to hate living with her parents, detesting their lifestyle. She wished for a place of her own, one where she could be away from the proximity of taverns. It got to be a game of sorts, that as she would climb the stairs to her parents door, she would sing (silently): "I hate this place—I hate this place"—over and over. She knew, without a doubt, she hated what was supposed to be her 'home'. The arguments that year had escalated to new heights! Memories of how her brother had been treated (MIS-treated?) came to her mind more and more often. It seemed so strange to her, that when she had been living a somewhat 'wild' life, frequenting taverns, dating the 'wrong' sort, her parents had never seemed the least interested in her whereabouts. Yet, after proving herself to be on the right track, and really applying herself to both school and work, now they chose this time to ridicule and nag her. Why now? She wondered. Then she realized she would soon be graduated and was that what threatened them? Would she not be paying as much as another Boarder might? Could her room become a money-making one, such as Everett's had? Possibly, she thought. Whatever the reason, the atmosphere was really becoming intolerable. In the forties young women did not strike out on their own, it was really unheard of, but how she yearned to do just that!

Thoughts of her brother were in her mind frequently. She seldom heard from him now, only a postcard from one far off place or another. She was aware he had divorced and remarried. His first marriage having ended after the loss of their two-year-old daughter to leukemia. He was heading for Japan she knew, but was reluctant to write him at this point, because what could she tell him?! Mostly she wrote of mundane things, knowing there wasn't much he could do to help her. Spiritually, she hurt deeply for her act, and prayed for forgiveness on a daily basis. She began attending church regularly once again, and felt better for it. Feeling really in control of her life, and trying to make something of herself, she couldn't understand her parents finding fault with her more and more often. Problems with her mother, especially seemed always to be present. One Friday she returned from school, went into her room and discovered it looked strange, then suddenly she knew why. Whenever she had gone to dances in the past, she had been given lovely dance cards, or bids. They would sometimes have braided silk ribbons, or lovely pictures displayed, they were really beautiful mementos. Inside were the different names of her dance partners. She had taken the collection and inserted them in a circle around the mirror on the dresser. Now though, they were gone! She went out to the kitchen to ask where they were only to be told they were "where they belonged-in the trash!!" "But why?" she asked disbelievingly, "Why would you throw them away? They were mine! You had no right!" Her mother turned quickly at that, and advised Shirley she had "every right!" This was her house, had she forgotten that?! It got so, Shirley would try to hide little notes or memoirs in her sock drawer, or in her pajamas, only to find them found and gone! It seemed Shirley would not be keeping anything her mother did not approve of. When, in desperation, she turned to her father for his understanding, it was always the same response: "Do as your mother says . . ." It was like a litany, repeated over and over. She once lost her temper, and tearfully asked him: "Why, just once, won't you listen to me?" that was when the new litany began: "Little girl, if you don't like the way things are here, you know where the door is!" Shirley must have heard that particular line hundreds of times, over and over. So as she continued to work hard at school and her job she also began to work at thinking of a means of 'escape'! But how?!

That March Doris and Red were married, although she couldn't graduate until June, nor turn eighteen until August, she was nevertheless a married woman! Shirley was in the wedding party, but still found it hard to grasp that her friends were now a married couple!

In May she turned 18 and was looking forward to graduation the next month. One Saturday afternoon at lunch time, one of the office girls and Shirley had chosen to walk over to Kelvyn Park to eat their lunch. As they strolled down the path, they noted a tall, good looking young man with a golf club, practicing putting on a slope. As they passed him, he looked up smiled, then staring at Shirley said: "I know you!" Rather surprised, Shirley responded: "You do?" "Yes, you are the one who used to correspond to all the servicemen from the factory where my mom, Gladys K. works right?" Laughing, Shirley replied: "Guilty!! But how did you know it was me?" "Well, mom described you quite well and knew your name, so I looked up my old high school book, and there you were. I kind of remembered seeing you in Kelvyn's halls when I was still in school, so it wasn't hard to put together." Although he seemed anxious to talk further, Shirley and Jean had to get back to the office, their lunch hour about over. So, with a smile and a wave they left, hearing him call out he'd be talking to her soon. Shirley dismissed his words and soon as she returned to her work, all thoughts of him were gone. The following week, however, when once again Jean and she walked through the park they met him again. He called out, with obvious delight, and walked over to say a few words. Jean and Shirley were polite enough, responding to his friendliness, but again left to return to work. These meetings occurred several times during the warm spring months, then one day he amazed her by phoning her at work. She was surprised and told him so. He explained that each time they had spoken Jean had always been present and he didn't want to appear rude, so decided the only way to speak to her privately was by telephone! He asked her out, for dinner and a movie, and although she laughed appreciatively, refused nevertheless. She still was fearful of her own reactions and ever mindful that she would not go back to being "the old Shirley" again. If she didn't date, she didn't drink, if she didn't drink she felt the chances of her getting involved in a sexual relationship were to her benefit. She was sure the only answer she could give was: "Thanks, but no thanks", which is what she did.

Meantime the situation between her and her parents began to worsen even more. The closer the time of graduation came the worse things became between the three. She had been told for so very long how stupid and inadequate she was, she had halfway begun to believe it, yet she'd proven herself at her job, hadn't she? Now the thought of getting away entertained her mind most of each day, still she could come up with no solution. Then, one day she returned from school and walked into the unlocked apartment, which was strange she thought. Standing by the door, she felt it was a bit too quiet, still she didn't call out, just made her way to her bedroom. She felt sure her mother must be home, else why would the door have been unlocked? She put one foot inside her bedroom and looked across the room with total shock . . . there, up against HER closet door was one of the men she recognized from downstairs, pressed against her mother! She let out a scream, then just stood there and gaped, as he zippered his pants. Her mother, pulling her skirt down, squeezed from behind him and approached Shirley, who had begun to shake violently, and was completely out of control. As her mother neared her she could see her lips moving but could hear nothing she was saying due to this loud piercing noise in her ears. Ignoring Shirley's attempt at holding her off, her mother put her hand across Shirley's mouth, and only then did Shirley realize the noise had been coming from her! Pushing her mother's hands away, she backed out of the room, still shaking, tears running down her face. Her mother kept saying things, but Shirley could not, would not, allow the word into her consciousness. Then Rose turned and said something to the man, and with one more look at Shirley, he nodded and left. When Rose moved toward Shirley once again, she tore loose and ran into the bathroom, the only room in the apartment with a lock on it. There she sat, and cried herself dry.

Eventually, of course, she had to leave that sanctuary and when she did, she unthinkingly headed for her bedroom. As she crossed the threshold and looked toward the end of the room, her eyes were drawn toward the closet. Her mind played a horrible trick on her, because once again, she saw them . . . her mother and Vern! She backed out of the bedroom into the dining room where she saw her schoolbooks strewn across the floor, where she must have dropped them. Bending down, she scooped them into her arms and turned, only to walk straight into her mother, standing very straight, feet apart, arms across her chest . . . waiting!

Shirley tried to look up, into her face, but simply couldn't do it. She put her head down and tried to walk around her mother, going into the kitchen, she supposed, she really didn't know where she should go. Her mother put her hands out, took hold of Shirley's arm and very quietly told her to put the books on the dining room table and get out to the kitchen and set the table for supper. Shirley couldn't believe her ears! Eating supper was about the last thing on her mind. Rose repeated her command, and once again, mechanically, Shirley did as she was told. As she finished putting the silverware out, she glanced at the clock, knowing it was about time for her father to come home from work. Rose saw her, and immediately came toward her, leaning across the length of the table from where Shirley stood. Slowly she told Shirley to go back into the bathroom, wash her face and comb her hair so she would look presentable, then she added: "Oh, and by the way, in case you have any ideas of telling your father all the things you IMAGINED, just forget it, because he will know you are lying and you will only get yourself in trouble again!" Shirley shook her head, but knew it would take more than a headshake to clear her thoughts. Slowly she headed for the bathroom, do to 'as she was told' yet again. When she looked into the mirror to comb her hair, she didn't see herself looking back. Instead she saw someone who had reached the end of doing as she was told. She knew, somehow, she was going to get out of this household no matter what it took! Looking at her mirror image she made that vow!

Soon her father came home, where Rose met him at the door as usual, taking his lunch box and stating that supper would be ready in a few minutes. As he walked past Shirley he stopped and looked at her face, then asked: "Is something wrong? Don't you feel well? You look terrible, are you sick?" Inside her head the words formed: "Oh, yeah, I'm sick alright, sick of living like we do . . . making believe we are a 'normal, loving family, when . . . ." But before a sound could come from her lips her mother was between them, pushing her husband down the hall, telling him to change clothes, didn't he hear her say supper was nearly ready . . . and so the moment passed. As she turned to the kitchen with a triumphant smile, Shirley knew she would never say anything to him, her mother had won yet again. Anything she said would only be twisted and turned around to be used against her, same as in the past. She knew now, she had to get away, and remembered her vow before the mirror. It was just a matter of time, now.

Somehow, the days melted one into the other and another week passed. Graduation was past, and it was Friday, payday, thought Shirley with a smile. When she returned from work, having cashed her check, she handed her mother her $15.00 Board money and was stunned to have her mother throw the bills on the table. With a sneer she said: "Oh, no you don't! Did you really think you were going to get away with a measly $15.00 a week for all I do for you? Listen big shot graduate, you try waking up to the real world why don't you? How do you think you would manage alone? There are meals to be made and laundry to be done. Everything costs money so you best think about turning your check over to me and I'll give you $5.00 a week, which should be plenty spending money for you. Now that you are out of school you shouldn't have anything to spend money on." Shirley didn't think-she reacted! "I will not give you my check! I work hard for that money! I earn every penny of it and I will not give it to you!!" Of course, the next words out of her mother's mouth were the old familiar tune: "Oh? Well, we'll see what your father says about that!" So when her father did come home, Shirley quickly went to him with the idea that she would continue to pay room and board, but didn't think it was fair she turn her entire check over . . . . She was cut off in mid-sentence, with the same old litany: "Do as your mother says . . ." Shirley's mouth opened, the word "But—" was spoken, which only succeeded in activating the rest of the litany: 'If you don't like it, you know where the door is!' Stunned, Shirley could hardly believe it. She never said another word, after all, what was there to say?

That night, after they had gone downstairs in their ritual, Shirley got out of bed and slowly and methodically began putting together what she felt would allow her to make the beginning of a life. Within less than half an hour she had put the clothes she needed for work together in a small pile. Next, she looked round and realized how few things she really had. Her clothes, a few books, that was it. Then gathering together all the inner strength she could muster, she went to the telephone to make a call which might possibly change her entire life.

There was a man who worked at the local garage across the street from her apartment building, his name was Glen. He worked on everyone's vehicles, including her bicycle. He was a very handsome man and well liked downstairs (at the tavern) among the men and women both. Problem was, he was married. Although marriage in itself shouldn't have been a problem, the fact was, he was "seeing" another woman. Now his wife never came along with him downstairs, nor did she attend the baseball games that were played among the many local taverns each weekend of the summer. However, Vivian ("the other Woman") often did. To her face, everyone treated her well, even friendly, but behind her back? That was another story! She was talked about as being the one in the wrong. For years Shirley had witnessed this little drama carried on, and never quite understood the attitudes. As for herself, she of course, liked Glen very much. He had taught her how to change a tire and to put air in her own tires so her bike could take her on wonderful rides. He was always very kind to her and a bit of a hero from the time she had first met him at the age of twelve. Thing was, she liked Vivian even more, although it was a period of time before she actually understood the situation of the threesome. Shirley had always made it a point to stand near Vivian or sit next to her at the ballgames. She was a lovely woman, truly quite beautiful, in face as well as figure. She was always dressed well, which probably made the other women feel shabby, but she never seemed to notice. As Shirley had gotten older she wondered if it wasn't a defense mechanism of sorts, on her part, because surely those house-wifely women (Rose, chief among them) with their 'holier than thou attitudes' tried always to keep her in her place . . . without uttering a word. Perhaps dressing as she did, always well-groomed, lovely as she was, was her only defense against them.

All this, is to explain the phone call Shirley made that eventful evening. She reached out to Vivian for help and never knew exactly why. Maybe she sensed in Vivian the 'maverick' in herself?! Fact was she needed a place to run to, and Vivian's apartment was only a block away, a block closer to Shirley's job. It seemed to be the ideal answer to Shirley, but she had no idea what Vivian's take would be. First, she apologized for calling so late, it was after 10 p.m., but was assured that time was no problem, what could she do for her? "Oh Boy! What can she do for me?", thought Shirley, "she could give me a way out of a very unhappy life and quite possibly put me on the first plateau of creating a new one." Later, Shirley never was able to recall how she finally did mange to blurt out her need for a place to say. Breathlessly, she waited for a response. Vivian, quietly, and in control, asked: "How old are you, honey? I sure can't afford to get in any trouble with the law." Shirley assured her that though she had just graduated, she had turned 18 the month before. Vivian asked if she were really sure this was what she wanted to do, was this just a snap decision? Shirley explained this was not just one little family spat, this had been an ongoing family war and she truly needed to get out as soon as possible. There were more questions, including the statement that if Shirley's mother didn't like her now, if she were to find out she was opening her home to her daughter she would really be on the spot! Shirley, sensing success, promised no one, her parents nor anyone else would ever know from her. She promised, further, that as soon as it was humanly possible she would find a place of her own. She had a good job, money saved up which should allow for her to make it on her own. At last, although Shirley sensed some reluctance on her part, Vivian said two wonderful words: "Alright, come." Then softly, she added: "before you walk out that door, you make sure you are mentally positive this is the path you want to take, because it won't be easy, believe me." Instinctively, Shirley knew she was speaking from her own experience, yet she quickly assured her she would be there soon, and hung up the telephone. She fairly floated to her room, her heart finally beginning to beat normally once again. "At last!", she thought, "at last!" Then she put on paper the words she had held in her mind for such a long time: 'You are always telling me if I don't like the way things are, I know where the door is. You are right, I do know where the door is, and I am walking through it, to a new and better life!' She propped the note up on her pillow and walked away.

Vivian welcomed Shirley as though she really meant it, and Shirley was warmed by her words. She was shown her room and invited to come back into the living room when she had her things put away. As she put her clothes in the closet and then into the dresser drawers she couldn't help but see her reflection in the mirror. Staring, she looked at herself and realized she was absolutely beaming! She felt so free! Finally she started toward the door, when she heard lovely music coming from the other side. Hesitating, she stepped into the living room to see Vivian seated at the piano, playing a hauntingly lovely melody. She hadn't known that aside from her beauty, Vivian also had such a talent. She sank into the couch, mesmerized by the scene and sounds. Soon, too soon, Vivian turned to find Shirley sitting there, and embarrassed put her hand to her mouth and apologized, hoping she hadn't disturbed her. Laughing aloud, Shirley said she had so enjoyed the music, she was fearful of disturbing her! Vivian and Shirley talked into the early morning hours and while Shirley told her of the unhappiness of her life, she never told her about her mother and Vern, later she wondered if it was because she was protecting Rose, or because she was just so ashamed of her mother.

The next week, an opportunity came quite unexpectedly, in the form of a co-worker, named Edna. Jean wasn't at work that day, so Shirley chose not to walk to the park, but instead sat with some of the other office workers. In sitting next to Edna, she couldn't help but note what an appetizing lunch she had before her! Reaching for her own dull sandwich she smiled at Edna and commented on it. Edna, in her delightful way, smiled and said that it probably looked special because she hadn't made it! "What? If you didn't, who did?", Shirley asked. Edna explained that after her father had died her mother had come to live with her and her husband, and it was she who made up their lunches each day. Shirley thought that sounded so sweet, and said so, rather wistfully. Picking up on her attitude, Edna asked if Shirley didn't live home with her mother, as well? Briefly Shirley explained she no longer lived with her parents, but sharing an apartment with a friend. Edna commented on how nice it was two friends could share living quarters, and so realizing she had misled her, clarified the situation. She explained her friend actually rented the place and she was just staying until she could make permanent arrangements. Problem was, she explained, she had to rely on walking and needed a place close to work, so she was looking for just that. Edna brightened and said where she lived there was a small neighborhood newspaper and she would keep an eye out for a place. Lunchtime being over, Shirley thanked her, and worried that perhaps she shouldn't have shared such a personal part of her life with a co-worker. She chewed her lip the rest of the afternoon.

Two days later, Edna approached Shirley and handed her a page from a newspaper. Shirley looked at her questioningly but before she could ask, she was told to read the circled part. As Edna seated herself at her desk, Shirley looked down at the paper she held in her hand. Sure enough, there was a large circled area, and to Shirley's joy it was an ad for: "Young woman wanted, sleeping room only. Must have references. $12.00 per week." Shirley looked across the office at Edna who gave her a wink and a large smile!

Stunned, Shirley could not believe it was possible that she could actually rent a room for less than she had to pay her mother, and have privacy to boot! She could barely wait until lunch hour when she could question Edna further. Where was this address? If it was too far, she worried, she would have to get up mighty early to catch the streetcar . . . still, even if this didn't work out, she realized there was a way to get out on her own after all. Looking up at the clock she urged its hands to move, move faster!

Edna was just as excited to speak to Shirley as it turned out, because she headed right toward her at noon. The pair sat away from the others while Edna explained that the ad had been placed by an elderly couple who lived two doors from her! She said she would be more than happy to give Shirley a referral, in fact would even go with her if she chose. Not wanting to sound like the Devil's advocate, Shirley had to explain the problem of logistics, explaining if the distance was too great—but before she could say anything further, Edna reached for her hand and said: "No, wait, there's more, let me tell you of my idea." Still holding onto Shirley's hand, as she continued on, Shirley realized Edna was indeed, a friend, more than a co-worker. It seemed that Edna's husband dropped her off each morning then drove on to his job a few blocks away, and to Edna's way of thinking there was no reason why he couldn't do the same for Shirley! Her eyes began to tear up as it began to dawn on her this was the answer to her many prayers. Ah, but there was even more, Edna had asked her mother if she would also make up a lunch for Shirley each day as she did for her and Casey, and her mother agreed. So for a few dollars a week a lunch and a ride would be possible, now the ad had only to be answered! Edna suggested Shirley ride home with them that evening, and answer the ad then and there. That was one of the longest days she had spent at the office, Shirley thought. Because she enjoyed her job so much the days usually went by quickly. Finally though, it was time to leave, and she followed Edna to the parking lot where her husband greeted both with a smile. How lucky she is, thought Shirley, watching them from the back seat, no, she corrected herself, how lucky they both are!

A short time later Shirley found herself looking into a large, old, oval shaped mirror hung above an antique dresser. Reflected in that mirror on one side, was a lovely brass bed with a goose-down type quilt looking as inviting as could be, in the center was a reflection of a happy young woman, with a hopeful expression on her face. As she stared back, she became aware of the elderly woman smiling so sweetly at her, also reflected in that mirror. As Shirley turned to face her, with her face enveloped in smiles, she breathed: "You like it, don't you?" Smiling back, Shirley replied: "Oh yes! I surely do." "Well, good then, and you don't feel $12.00 is too high?" "Oh my, no" Shirley responded, "It will be just fine." Shirley explained she couldn't move in until the weekend, as she had to move out from where she was staying and she was assured that would be no problem. Handing her the ten and two dollar bills, which had wilted from her sweaty palms, she quite literally held her breath until she had gotten a receipt. As she prepared to leave, she was informed they really did need to speak on a few matters. Whereupon she was cautioned that there would be no company (young men) in her room, but she could arrange to use their parlor on occasion, and also she should feel free to use the kitchen to prepare breakfast for herself. (How ironic, thought Shirley, I couldn't even use my parents' parlor!) But the fact that she would be able to boil water for instant coffee or tea was great news, because she could pick up a donut, or some such snack which would keep her until lunchtime when a delicious lunch would be eaten courtesy of Edna's mother. Oh, life was good!

Before boarding the streetcar to return to Vivian's Shirley stopped for a quick supper, then picked up a bottle of Vivian's favorite perfume, asking the clerk to gift-wrap it. When she entered the apartment, Vivian looked up from her reading with a welcoming smile, but something must have shown on Shirley's face, because she seemed to know that something was in the wind. Smiling, she quickly put her book aside and motioned Shirley to join her on the couch. As Shirley neared her, she placed the small wrapped package in Vivian's hands with a smile of her own. She took the package, looked down at it, but made no move to open it, her eyes seemed to glisten. Softly she said: "You're leaving aren't you? You aren't going back." her voice broke, "home, are you?" Quickly, Shirley hastened to assure her that was surely not her intent, then she told of the room she had found. She told her too, of what a haven she had given, and wanted so much for her to know how much it was appreciated. Vivian looked at Shirley, fondly, and told her that she had been good for her, as well. Because she had realized how strong Shirley had to be to have made such a big move at her tender age, and she too, was now going to be strong. Vivian went on to say that she had decided to move to another state, but wanted to be sure that Shirley was settled and safe before she even mentioned it! A stunned Shirley stammered: "But, I don't understand, I mean what about . . . about Glen, you know", she hesitated over the up to now, never spoken name. Vivian reached out and took Shirley's hand in hers, and as the tears trickled down her cheeks, she told Shirley how she had given her situation so very much thought the past weeks. She had noticed how Shirley would steer clean of any reference to Glen, though she knew she was aware of their relationship. She went on to say that at last she had truly come to terms with her life, and was certain Glen would never be able to offer her anymore than what they had shared over the years. Their religion would not allow for Glen and his wife to go their separate ways and Vivian had come to understand she had to make a leap of faith. She realized that the relationship had kept her from having a full and complete life. Then, seeing Shirley, starting out from scratch, made her know that she too, could start over. "But not here", she said, as the old Vivian Shirley knew sat up, back straight, and with the start of the old defiant smile on her lips. "No, not anywhere near here. I have a sister in California", she continued, "and for years she has been urging me to come for more than the weeks I have spent there in the winter, and so I have decided to do just that!" Shirley stared at her in amazement as she asked: "But what about all your lovely furniture here, and your piano . . . oh, yes, your piano?" So often the past couple of weeks Shirley had heard through her closed door, Vivian playing sad but beautiful melodies on her beloved piano. Then Vivian DID smile! "Oh, my dear, didn't you know that furniture can be moved as well as people? But of course, most of my things will move with me, and you, a piece of you will always be with me in my heart, as well. Because you really opened my eyes, I will always be grateful." The two friends embraced each other with strong and mixed feelings, knowing they would probably not see each other again. After sharing her plans, Shirley went to her room and Vivian to hers both unable to speak any further.

Shirley was scarcely able to sleep that night, her emotions were so high. With a new place to live, her life beginning to undergo many changes, and now, losing

Vivian to distance was almost more than she could bear! But even as her cheeks became wet from tears she couldn't control, she realized, deep inside, even with the sadness of such a loss there was joy too! For how long had she yearned to leave her parents? For how long had she sought the answer as to how? Now, at last, things were beginning to fall into place, and she must thank God for that. As she began to pray, her eyes closed and she fell into a restful sleep after all.

The following day, after work, Shirley was busy getting her belongs together, for Edna and her husband had offered to move her with their truck, when Vivian tapped on the door. She was urged to come in, the door hadn't even been closed in the anxiety of getting things done. She perched on the side of the bed, and said she had something she wanted Shirley to have, but she would rather it not be opened until she were settled into her new place. Shirley looked at her questioningly, but nodded in agreement as she took the large envelope and placed it on top of her pile of clothing. Soon everything was once again ready to be put into her faithful shopping bags, with a few more articles she had gotten since, they were filled to the top. She took one, Vivian the other and with her coat and purse over her arm, Shirley looked back to what she'd termed her 'haven' and said her farewell in her mind. As the two stood there, looking at one another, words were difficult to come by. Finally, they simply embraced and wept their soft farewells in unison. As she climbed into Casey's truck she saw Vivian lift her arm to wave and their eyes locked, and once again the tears flowed. That evening, sitting in her quaint old bed she opened the enveloped, it was a beautiful letter, with a $100.00 enclosed 'to help her get started,' it read! That was a great deal of money in 1946, and between grasping that thought and the meaningful words written, it was almost more than she could bear. Seemed it was once again time to thank the Lord.

Soon Shirley's life settled into a most calm and pleasing kind of monotony! Due to the small amount of rent, paying a minimum amount for her lunches five days a week, and most often riding home with Edna, she quickly found she could save money. Finally, one Saturday she made a big decision, she went to open up her own bank account so that she might begin to look toward an even better future. In church the next morning, she really felt the deep need to give thanks more than ever.

A few days later, her outside line rang, which was surprising as most of the friends she now had, were also co-workers. Even more surprising was the voice on the other end! "Is that you, Shirley? It's mother!" Nearly a year had gone by, yet the fearful tingling immediately passed through her as she sat with the telephone in hand. Not sure she wanted to take part in this call, she simply held her breath and waited. "Shirley? Are you there? Operator? came through to her. In a fearful voice she said: "Yes, mother, it's me . . . what's wrong?" (Fearing the worst.) "Why, nothing is wrong", she was informed, in a cheerful voice that had always been reserved for her friends, not family and certainly not Shirley. "No, nothing is wrong here, how are things with you?" Shirley was glad she couldn't see her face, matter of fact she was glad on one else could either! She felt her cheeks burning as she huddled over her worktable, so no one would hear her end of the conversation. Finally, in a terse voice, she said: "What is it you want, mother, I am at work you know, and we are not allowed to have personal calls." (This probably wasn't even true, but she hadn't really put it to the test, having never had but one call-from the 'golfing guy' as she had come to think of him-from Kelvyn Park.) She only knew that she was not yet prepared to chit chat with 'the enemy' at that point in time. Her mother questioned why, if she wasn't to receive calls that she was able to get in touch with her, besides, since she had no idea where she was living these days what else could she do?! Over her shoulder Shirley saw her boss heading toward her, with a sheaf of papers in his hand, so knowing the call would have to be cut short she agreed to calling back after work and quickly hung up. That evening she told Edna she would not be riding home with her as she had some business to take care of. She then took herself to a nice restaurant and had dinner, building her stamina, while she rehearsed what she would say when she returned her mother's call. Afterward, using the restaurant's phone booth, she made the call, dreading what was to come. After ringing several times the telephone was finally answered, but it was her father's voice she heard! Chills literally took over her body and she quickly hung up. As she stood there in the phone booth trying to sort out her reaction, she knew she had to postpone that call until she had taken more time to think things out. Next day, after a fretful night, she walked to a public telephone during her lunch hour, and called her mother, knowing it was Friday, she would be home. She was. She sounded quite pleased to hear Shirley's voice and never questioned why she hadn't called the day before as promised. They talked for a few minutes about generalities, the weather, and the fact she was eating lunch and talking to her at the same time, which prompted her mother to ask her to lunch "someday". Explaining that her lunch hour didn't really allow enough time to make it to her place, eat and get back, she thanked her anyway. Then came another shocker! "Well, then, how about coming over for dinner next Sunday?" Dipping into her ready-excuses she quickly said she was busy Sunday. Not taking a minute the response was, "Well, then the following Sunday will be fine, why don't you come in the morning?" Shirley responded that she didn't get out of church until 11, so noon would probably be the soonest she could make it. A week from Sunday, at noon, was settled on, before she even realized she had agreed! Standing with the disconnected phone in her hand, she felt dazed, trying to figure out what had just happened!

For two weeks Shirley worried over that Sunday, knowing only that she had to look her best to keep her pride intact, no matter what. So that weekend she went to Logan Square and purchased a gray sharkskin suit, where she took it to the tailor so it might fit her perfectly. Next she purchased a Kelly green blouse with matching green (faux alligator) shoes and purse. The day came, too soon for Shirley's taste, but after dressing in her new outfit, she stood back and looked into that same old, oval mirror over the dresser and smiled. She saw the change that had come over her the past months. The young, hopeful girl, so unsure of herself, had changed into a grown, self-assured woman. She was pleased with what she saw and felt ready for whatever was to come. In church she prayed once again for God's strength to fill her, and once again knew she must forgive whatever her parents had done or said, because when we say the words of the Lord's prayer, we must mean them. To utter: "Forgive us . . . as we forgive others" has to be believed and practiced. For forgiveness to be granted, it must be given, yet she feared her lack of strength. "Help me, Lord, help me", she prayed.

Finding herself once again climbing the same stairs up to her folk's apartment, she recalled how she used to take step by step, while chanting to herself: "I hate this place, I hate this place . . ." over and over. As she raised her hand to rap on it, the door opened and there stood her mother with a look on her face Shirley found hard to read. Her mother simply backed away a few paces and said how glad she was that she was on time as dinner was nearly ready. As she followed her mother into the kitchen, she noted that it hadn't changed a bit, so she gingerly sat at her 'old place'. She watched as her mother scurried around the stove, with her father nowhere in sight, she presumed he was in the parlor. The kitchen table was set, still she asked if there was anything she could do, and nearly fell from the chair when she was told it would be nice if she would get the butter out, and oh, yes, open a can of olives and pour them in this dish. Though it was a surprise, it was also a relief to be asked to take part in a few of the preparations and it helped keep her mind occupied. Soon diner was ready and her mother called out to her husband to come and eat. Shirley was still standing as he came down the hall, she held her breath, without being aware of it, and waited. She didn't have to wait long, he came out, looked at Shirley, then slowly looked her up and down twice. Aware that she looked good, she foolishly expected to hear him say as much. Wrong! He gave her the strangest kind of half smile then sat down in his place at the table. Finally, still standing in the same spot, she let her breath out and looked from him to her mother, who waved her hand toward him as though to say "Pay no attention!", and simply told Shirley to sit down, so we can eat. If she'd had any thoughts of some big reconciliation taking place they sure melted quickly! The three ate in silence, just as in the past, and though her mother had always been a good cook, she could have served straw for all Shirley could taste. Once finished, her father returned to the parlor and Shirley stood to help clean off the table. She had hung her suit coat over the chair, and her mother handed her a big dishtowel, suggesting she might want to pin it around her, so as not to mess up her good clothes while helping with the dishes. She did just that, and soon found the two of them doing dishes together as they had so often in the past. "So, I know you're still working at the same place, you must like it, huh?" Because her job was the biggest part of her life, she took the bait quickly, and began explaining different aspects of her work. Soon they were conversing like two women, not friends, exactly, but surely not enemies, and yet, not quite like mother and daughter either! They talked about shopping and Shirley mentioned how she had developed the habit of going to the Logan Square area most weekends, not necessarily to buy anything, but to window shop. Her mother expressed surprise to find that she had been so close by, and they had not met. They even chewed at the possibility of meeting there one day, and eating lunch together. Surprising to herself, even that appealed to Shirley, because outside of work, she had made no real friends. Between the conversation and drying dishes, there was a calming effect so that she was surprised to find herself relaxed and actually beginning to enjoy herself! Suddenly, her father appeared, asking her to move, so he might get into the bathroom. She backed out of his way, and then a bit further, as he made it obvious he was avoiding any physical contact with her. When he re-entered the kitchen Shirley was standing in the center of the room, removing the protective towel she'd wrapped about her waist. Looking up, she saw once again that same strange half smile she'd seen earlier. So pulling herself up straight, looking right at him she said her first words directly to her father: "What is it? What are you smiling about?" He looked back at her and stated quite matter-of-factly: 'I am not smiling, young lady, it is just that the very fact the way you show up here, all dressed up, proves what I thought all along." Despite not wanting the words to leave her lips she heard herself responding. "What you always thought? What do you mean?" With a sneer he spit out: "Isn't it obvious? You and Everett are more alike than you know. He left, and turned out to be nothing but a thief, and you—you are even worse!" Shaking her head, she slowly answered him: "Everett is no thief! My God, he's serving his country. He's in the Air Corps, you should be proud of him, because I sure am!" Then came the final blow! "What makes you think anyone would care what YOU think?! You . . . dressed up like a tramp! The only reason you wanted to leave here is so you could sleep around and get men to buy you outfits like that, I just . . . ." As they stood, confronting one another, the ring of the telephone shattered the air. Giving one last venomous look at Shirley, he turned on his heels and picked up the phone with a harsh: "Hello!" Then as she and her mother stood silently watching, she saw this terrible look come over his face. He looked across the room at Shirley, and with the most triumphant of looks, holding the phone out at arms length, he said: "It's for YOU! Another one of your men!!" Dropping the phone he left the room. Startled, she walked over and picked up the telephone. She had not lived in this apartment for nearly a year, and the first time she enters she gets a phone call?! She could not begin to imagine who it would be, as she hesitantly mumbled a "Hello?" "Hello, yourself!" came a vaguely familiar voice over the wire. "Remember me? Frank? You know, from Kelvyn Park . . . the golfer!" As she stood there, trying to think, her father entered the room and their eyes met. Anger! She had never felt such terrible anger! The anger filled her mind and her throat so she could barely breathe. Finally, after prompting from Frank: "Are you there? Are you there?" she took a huge breath and answered: "Yes, yes, I AM here, but THAT Is what is so strange! I am here, but I have not BEEN here for some months and then for you to call when I am, well, it just seems strange, that's all. "Yeah, well, maybe it is strange to you, but to me, Shirley it's an omen!" Distracted she asked what he was talking about, conscious that her father was standing there, absorbing every word she uttered. "Well, last time I asked you out, you said thanks but no thanks and now I feel this must be an omen that you are going to say 'yes' to seeing me. So, what do you say? I can be there in ten minutes!" Knowing full well she might regret this show of defiance, of independence, she nevertheless responded with: 'Yeah, sure, why don't you come by and pick me up?" Then she added as meaningful as possible, staring right at her father: "You remember where my parents live, don't you . . . above the tavern?" Then, recalling how her dates had never been allowed to pick her up but had been required to come up the stairs and knock on the door "like gentlemen", she quickly added: "You needn't come up, I'll be waiting for you downstairs!" Then hanging up the phone, she turned to her father and said: "Thank you so much, for not letting me miss out on a date!", then literally prancing past him went to the kitchen. She told her mother: "Thank you for the tasty dinner but I must leave now, it would seem my father is uncomfortable in my presence, besides I have a date!" Her mother did not argue the point, but walked Shirley to the door and reminded her once again that they must meet for lunch—soon.

Standing on the sidewalk, outside the apartment door, waiting for Frank's car to pull up she realized she had put her foot in her mouth by accepting this meeting. Still, she was so filled with anger with her father and his filthy insinuations, she had no thought of backing out, sure she was being watched from the upstairs window. Childishly she hoped Frank would not show up in some old, beat-up junk! However, when he pulled to the curb minutes later, in a beautiful, new 98 Oldsmobile, she was impressed, but when he jumped out and assisted her into the car she was really impressed. As they pulled away from the curb she couldn't keep from smiling up at the window above, where she saw the livid face of her father staring down. No matter what, she promised herself, that exit I just made has made it all worthwhile! Smiling to herself, at her 'victory' of sorts, she found the car had stopped. Looking out she saw they were in front of one of the neighborhood hangouts for the young. Entering she met and greeted many old friends. Soon she found herself in a booth, drink in her hand, laughing and determined to forget the last hour.

Later, when Frank offered to drive her home, she felt it only made good sense to accept, and so he soon pulled up in front of the old home where she rented her room. He asked to come in, but of course, she hid behind words, saying she was "not allowed" to have guests. She explained she was only renting a sleeping room. He accepted this, and over the next weeks, called her regularly, at work, and took her to dinner and the movies. More and more they seemed to be quite compatible. It had been sometime since she had been with a member of the opposite sex, aside from fellow office workers. It was especially exciting, dating one on one, an exhilarating experience. After several dates, his arm hung over the back of the car seat and he kissed her, a gentle undemanding kiss, and Shirley was warmed by his respectful attitude. She thought how strange that she had met this really nice young man (he was three years older than she) all because she was trying "to show" her father! The more time they spent together, the more fond of him she became. The fact he lived home with his parents did not surprise her, and he brought her there often. Most times only his mother was present and she and Shirley seemed to hit it off fine. They often spent time reminiscing about the solder factory where they had met, and where Gladys still worked. She often thought aloud, how strange it was, that while she had showed Shirley his service photo, and had wished for her to meet "Buddy" Shirley had left the plant before that had come about. Yet, they had met and she insisted it had to be 'fate'. At times, Shirley felt overwhelmed by her enthusiasm, yet she was flattered at the same time. Seeing how close the mother and son seemed to be, she was surprised at being swept into a relationship she was still unsure of herself. Many Sunday's Shirley would spend with Bud and his parents, having dinner, playing pinochle. She was always made to feel a part of their family. And as always, it was the old yearning for a family that touched her so. She knew that they were accepted as "a couple" by their friends, and yet the old self-doubt returned. At night, alone in her bed, she began to think that everyone else probably knew better than she, how well-suited they were to each other. Then one evening, parked in front of that old house once again, having just returned from a pleasant time with his parents, Bud took her in his arms and asked her to marry him! Shirley, still so unsure of herself, was speechless. Finally, being pressed for an answer, she begged off, saying she needed time to think. Bud looked so hurt, his head down he said he couldn't understand what there was to think about. He said he loved her, didn't she care for him as well? Shirley knew she wanted a full life, to have children she could love, but married? To Bud? Now? She told him of her misgivings about the amount of time they spent in taverns, with 'the crowd.' She told of how uncomfortable she felt about this, unable to look into his face, fearing his reaction. Frank reached out, taking her in his arms and saying it was perfectly normal for her to feel that way, after all she had told him of the amount of time her parents spent drinking 'downstairs'. He managed to soothe her with promises of how things would be different for them. They were young, they could make a wonderful life—together—have a family. She had only to give him a chance—please! So she agreed to do just that.

Although, he insisted he didn't care if Shirley was a Catholic, he said he simply would not attend church with her. This, due to his father, who was supposedly a Catholic, but had surely let Bud down, as a parent. Coming from the Count of Cork, Ireland with the grand name of Francis Hilary, Shirley knew very little about him from the few hours they had spent together. Because Shirley had made her commitment to him, Bud shared his family history with her as well, and it wasn't a pretty story either. Bud had been raised by his mother and an aunt, who had led him to believe, as a child, that his father was dead. One day he returned from high school at the age of 15, to find a strange man sitting in the living room. His mother informed him that this was his father! Where he had been all this time, what had happened, how this event had come to be, was never explained to him. It was the way it was then, children were simply told what to do and what not to do and just accept it, as the way it was to be. Shirley could understand that as well, knowing the way her own parents had been so secretive about their backgrounds. She never knew they had both been married before, until the departure of Everett, when it was rationally 'explained' to her that he was not her brother. So Bud's confusion and dismay was understood by her as well. He was simply expected to accept this new situation, to see this man, who drank heavily, hugging his beloved mother was almost more than he could stand to bear. This turn of events plus the war itself, led to Bud enlisting in the Air corps.

Being in the war, seeing combat, still carrying shrapnel in his shoulders and back, he came home a man, no longer a young boy, more capable of accepting. Many times, after picking Shirley up at work, Bud and she would pick up his father at a local tavern as well. After dropping his father off, the couple would go on their own way. It still seemed astounding to Shirley to see such affection displayed between Bud and his mother. It was so obvious she loved him deeply, she made every effort to show him. She would wait on him, and hover over him, taking care of whatever wishes he had. When Shirley was present he would simply extend his wants 'for us' and she seemed always willing to do for them both. Shirley thought that at last she had become part of a loving family, much as Doris had, and she was thankful. With all this in mind, she knew it was foolish to worry about Bud not wishing to be married in the Church. Rather, they told his parents how they planned on being married by a judge, "with just our families present" Bud ended. "Our families?" echoed in Shirley's mind, they had never discussed that before, she would have to speak to him later, when they were alone. Later, she broached the subject and was told that this was one thing Bud said he felt strongly about. He thought they should go to her parents, together, and inform them of their love and marriage intentions, so sure was he that all would work out well. Of course, Shirley was quite dubious about the whole plan, but, as usual, went along with it, feeling what would be—would be, and she had nothing to lose! She telephoned her mother and asked if she might 'stop by', there was a moment of silence, then she asked: "What is it? Don't tell me you are in some trouble?" Unsure of how to reply, Shirley simply said she had to hang up now, being at work, but would be there Friday evening. The next Friday Bud picked her up from work, and they drove to her parents as planned. As she ascended those hated stairs once again, there were butterflies in her stomach. She hadn't realized how very much she wanted the whole scenario to come out as Bud had painted it. About to knock on the door, she wondered if she looked as apprehensive as she felt, then she felt Bud's hand on her shoulder as he gently prodded her with his smiling confidence. Taking his cue she pulled a smile out from somewhere deep inside herself and knocked as firmly as she could. Her mother opened the door, looked quickly at Shirley, then her eyes sought out this handsome young man standing behind her. She smiled up at him and stepping back, ushered them in, with her eyes never leaving his face. They stood there, the three of them, and she was at a loss as to what to do or say, but before she opened her mouth, Bud took over. Smiling, he took her mothers hand and introduced himself, as her obviously admiring eyes opened ever wider. Finally, she broke off her stare and glancing over her shoulder, at Shirley, with this almost incredulous look, guided them both into the front room. In all the years she'd lived there, the times she had been allowed in the front room were very few. Sometimes, on Sunday mornings after returning from church, she had been able to join her father and listen to the radio until dinner was ready. She was frankly, uncomfortable in this nearly unused room, and welcomed returning to the kitchen where her mother sat, or better still to her own room. As they entered the room her father slowly lowered the newspaper he was holding and looked up at Bud, with real interest. Shirley was secretly pleased that Bud was as handsome as he was, and having spent his stint in the Air Corps had taught him good posture as well as good manners and she knew he was making an impression on her parents. He was 6'2" tall to Shirley's 4'11", but no one had ever made her feel more pride in being tiny, than he did at that moment. He reached out to shake her fathers hand as she introduced him and said: "I am truly pleased to meet You, sir." Quickly, Rose stepped in and said: "Oh, please, sit down won't you? It sure is a pleasure meeting you too." Bud smiled at her and promptly took a seat on the sofa, looking completely at ease, while Shirley stood there, looking for all the world the outsider of the four! Ready to panic, she sought Bud's eye for reassurance, and he quickly patted the seat next to himself and said: "Sit, honey, sit!" Her father looked at her mother who was sitting there staring, admiringly at Bud, then to Bud, then to Shirley and asked, quite pleasantly: "Well, now, what is this visit all about?" Shirley felt her jaw wanting to drop to her chest as she recalled their last bitter confrontation. His kindly, parental attitude was hard to take in, but right then Bud leaned toward him and said: "Well, sir, truth is, I've come to ask for the hand of your daughter."

Silence! Complete and utter silence reigned as Shirley sat frozen in place, eyes closed tightly. Meanwhile, strange little whirlwinds were moving through her mind—thought fragments—going in many directions but stopping nowhere. Then suddenly she heard this rumble of noises, and felt movement, before she could open her eyes she felt her mothers arms around her as she joyfully cried out how happy she was for them! Through blurred vision she saw over her mothers shoulder her father and Bud, in what was almost an embrace! Hardly believing what was happening, she felt her wildest dreams had just come true! They actually were happy for her! They took turns hugging her and saying all the wonderful things she had dreamed she might hear. The best part was that they were including Bud in all this happiness as well. Bud's reaction? He was eating it up, just standing there, grinning at Shirley with an "I told you so" look! Soon, they settled back down and began talking of their future. Bud took the lead by telling of their plans to be married, and the date settled on was July 3rd, the say before Shirley's mothers birthday. Having been born of the 4th of July had always allowed for a big celebration and the insinuation was that the wedding would add to the festivities. It was also discussed that both sets of parents should meet and get to know one another, with Bud suggesting he have his mother call Rose for a specific date. Then, (not too surprisingly, thought Shirley) her father suggested they all four go downstairs and have a drink to celebrate the news! Soon, Shirley found herself seated on a barstool with Bud on one side and her father the other, while her mother, on the other side of Bud, kept him deep in conversation. She felt rather left out, but then censured herself, reminding herself that her life had taken a big turn for the good this day. Sometime during that strange evening it was decided that Shirley should return to her parents, so it would look proper, being married from there. Knowing it was for but a short time, Shirley was eased into agreeing for the next four months, how difficult could it be?!

The evening their mutual parents were to meet, things did not go as planned. In the interim Shirley had moved back into her old room, creating the respectable image her parents and Bud desired. Things had started out smoothly enough, with her being at work everyday, then she and Bud going out in the evenings, after which they would join her parents, downstairs, for a nightcap. With Bud there as the ever-present buffer, there were no arguments. Then the evening all four parents were together there was enough arguing to make up for the peaceful times. Bud's mother insisted on things going HER way, and of course, Shirley's mother knew it should go HER way. When things really got bad, Shirley found herself reduced to frustrated tears. Bud simply took her arm, and led her out the door, where he turned and announced to the four rabble-rousers that he and Shirley were leaving . . . now! "It was OUR wedding, supposedly being arranged, and we will do our own arranging, thank you", and he closed the door. The two decided then and there that the July date was not to be, they drove to Chicago and were married there in the Courthouse. Afterward they drove to each of the parents and told them not to concern themselves about next July—because here is our wedding certificate, and it's only March! Bud and Shirley had put their money together and used it for a down payment on a cute little apartment they had found. They shopped for what furniture they would need right away. This taken care of, they left for a few days honeymoon, knowing they both had to return to their jobs within the five days left of their vacations. When they returned from Wisconsin they stopped at her parents so she might pick up her things to move into their apartment. When Rose met them at the door, she wore a strange look on her face, when asked what was wrong, she said: "Well, right after you left the woman who had rented you your apartment called. It seems her niece had need for the place now, and being family, she had no choice but to return YOUR deposit! It looks as though you don't have a place of your own after all!" This last was said with the strange smile on her face, and Shirley was stunned. Turning to Bud, she questioned: "What are we going to do now?" He seemed to be quite calm, she thought, strangely so, why isn't he as upset as I am? Finally, he spoke up and said that if it wouldn't be too much of an imposition, perhaps they could both stay there, in Shirley's old room. Speechless, Shirley just stood there in silence. She felt there wasn't much to say, because surely they would be laughed right out the door. When, to her shock, she heard her mother's quickly, enthused: "What a wonderful idea! Come in and let's talk about it!" Shirley couldn't believe her ears, then, nodding to her, Rose bade her to: "Go get your father, I'm sure he will be wanting to hear this, too." Dazed, she did as she was told, and soon her father appeared and joined in welcoming then back home. That night as she lay in bed, with Bud sleeping next to her, her mind was filled with confused thoughts. She could not accept the fact that she was back in the very place she had sought and worked so hard, to get away from! "Oh, god", she prayed, how could you let this happen?!"

The first days things went well, when she returned from work she would change clothes and help her mother get supper together. Within minutes of each other, Bud and her father would arrive and the four would sit down to dinner. Because she had never been allowed to speak during mealtime, she naturally did not instigate conversation. Having been scolded over the years, that she should eat, and refrain from her nonsense talk, it had stuck with her. Bud, on the other hand would talk non-stop. Strangely, her parents seemed to enjoy this change and Shirley mentally shrugged her not understanding away. When dishes were done, her parents would begin to prepare for the "ritual" and Bud would insist he and Shirley should join them. At first, it was almost fun to sit among all the people who had known her only as "Rosie and Shorty's daughter" and be accepted as a married woman—Bud's wife. But after one drink, which she sipped on, she was ready to go back upstairs, but Bud was always reluctant. It made for an uncomfortable situation. Things came to a head a couple weeks later, when her parents headed downstairs, early one Sunday afternoon, and Bud was pushing her to get ready and join them. But it was Spring, the weather was warming, she was young and she wanted to go to the park or go for a walk, anyplace actually, than down to that smelly tavern. Even as she was making her appeal, things suddenly went dark. She couldn't imagine what had happened. Finally, opening her eyes, they widened as she saw these strange forms swinging back and forth above her! Slowly she turned her head, and discovered she was inside their closet, sprawled on the floor, and those forms were coat hangers! Looking up, she saw Bud standing over her, with a clenched fist up to his chest and his mouth tight. "Get up! Get up and stop this faking!" He reached down and pulled her up to her feet. She stood there, wavering, trying to figure out what had just happened. Finally, she looked up into his face and, here he was, standing there with this soft, smile, patting her shoulder. She gasped: "What did you DO?" He didn't respond, he simply pushed her gently toward the bathroom advising her to wash her face so they could go downstairs. Haltingly, she went into the bathroom and looked into the mirror over the basin, the shocked face looking back at her, looked none the worse for wear. Her hair was mussed, but what had happened?, she wondered silently. Slowly, her mind began to accept the fact that Bud had struck her . . . hard! She rinsed her face in cool water and tried to get her thoughts together at the same time. Then, as she brushed her hair into place, she felt sharp pains, and knew why her face didn't look different, he had struck her on the side of the head! When she came out, there stood Bud, smiling easily, asking if she was ready. Shirley was stunned: "Ready? Ready for what? To have you sock me, whenever I don't want to do what you want? Are you crazy?" Slowly, the smile disappeared and he went to her, with actual tears coming down his face. On his knees he hugged her, and apologized over and over. He begged for forgiveness, he had no idea what had happened, but it would never happen again. Fool, that she was, because she wanted to, so badly, she believed him.

PART II

MARRIED LIFE

AFTER THE FRIGHTENING experience of being struck so hard she'd been knocked unconscious, Shirley had no idea how this Dream Marriage had taken such a turn. That day, after Bud held her, begging on his knee's that she forgive him . . . they went into their room and spent hours talking. He continued to profess his love for her, she finally came to believe he was telling the truth. He loved her, he loved her and had gotten her out of her parent's home, hadn't he? Wait, no, she was unhappily once again in their home, surely the last place she wanted to be. Instinctively she thought that the proximity of the tavern downstairs was not going to help matters, she'd have to do something. So even as Bud caressed her, and made love to her, her mind raced with the thought of leaving once again.

The next day, Shirley went to the office once again, and all her co-workers who had held an impromptu shower during their lunch hour teased her about her new status. She had been given many gifts for her new life, and she was embarrassed to realize she didn't really have a new life at all. Not yet, anyway, she amended, but soon, God willing, soon. When she returned from work her mother was fixing dinner and she changed her clothes and offered to help. As the two women worked side by side, seeming to compatible, Shirley thought maybe she should turn to her mother and tell her what had happened the day before. As she began to work up the nerve to approach the subject, her mother turned to her and asked why she and Bud had not joined them Sunday afternoon. It seemed the perfect time to tell her why, so slowly she said how she hadn't wanted to go downstairs, but out for a walk on such a nice day. With her hands on her hips Rose turned around abruptly and what did you do? "I didn't DO anything!" Shirley objected. "You don't understand—he hit me! Tearing up, she sobbed; "He hit me hard!" Her mother looked right at her and said she had brought it on herself! "You should have done what he wanted, and not have been so selfish! God, you are so stupid! I knew you'd mess this up too!", she ended her tirade. Shirley could hardly take it in, what had she expected, though? Certainly not any sympathy, she should have known better than even mentioning it. From now on, she promised herself she would keep everything to herself, and once again find a way to leave this place. Thankfully, Rose said nothing about their conversation, and the days slipped by one by one. Then one morning soon after, she awakened feeling strange, she couldn't put her finger on why, exactly, but something was wrong. That morning at work, Edna came over and told her she had brought some sweets her mother had baked, and they would all be sharing at lunchtime. Shirley smiled her thanks, and continued with her work, however when lunchtime arrived and she walked into the break room she felt her stomach lurch at the smells of the food! There would be no treats for her, in fact as she headed for the bathroom she was unsure if she could even stomach her lunch! She sat there for a few minutes, trying to recall what she might have eaten that would have upset her stomach so, then came the dawn! She had felt this way once before, hadn't she?! She was pregnant! Instead of feeling joy she felt fear! Would she have a healthy baby? Just then Edna came seeking her out, taking one look at Shirley, pale and shaky, she grabbed her shoulder and said: "Oh gosh! You're pregnant aren't you? Our young bride is going to be a mother! Oh, how wonderful! You must tell everyone, this is so exciting!" Still, trying to cope with her thoughts, Shirley said she needed time before making any announcements and so Edna relented—"for now" she said.

Later, as she walked home she was filled with wonder. Often that walk was the perfect time for her to talk with God. This day she knew she must give thanks that she was pregnant, she'd often wondered if she would be able to have a child. Now, she was quite sure, she was going to have one. Discreetly patting her tummy, she thought she must go to a doctor, make sure she was prepared for this new little life. Then the whole situation seemed overwhelming. She simply could not live with her parents, not now, they needed to be by themselves, she and Bud, and this new being they had created. She would tell Bud tonight, when they were alone, he had been her savior before, he could be again. That night when her parents headed downstairs, Shirley took Bud by the hand and sat him down on the edge of their bed. "I have news, wonderful news", she started out. "Oh Yeah? Smiling at her, Bud said: "And what would this new be—that's so wonderful?" Taking a breath she beamed: "YOU are going to be a daddy!" With a shocked face he asked: 'Are you sure?" "Yes I'm sure, I haven't been to a doctor yet, but I am sure, oh, Bud, we are going to be a family." He reached up and took her in his arms, with watery eyes he simply held her close, and whispered in awe, "I am so happy, when will the baby come? How soon? Oh this is wonderful news, you were right! Have you told anyone yet?" She said no, she hadn't told anyone, it was just that Edna had guessed! "You make an appointment with the doctor for Saturday, okay? Then I can drive you and be with you . . . this is so great!!" Relieved that he was so thrilled, Shirley slept well that night, after she thanked God, once again.

The doctor examined her and smilingly informed her, that she was indeed, pregnant and everything looked fine. Then he spoke with the two of them together, answering their questions, and giving them literature to read so they might know what precautions they need take, and what diet Shirley should follow. From what information Shirley had given him, and from his exam he gauged the baby should arrive early the next year—1948. What a new year this would be, they agreed.

From that day on, Shirley sought a way for them to find a place for themselves, without much luck. Then, one day, as fate would have it, she met an old friend from high school. They went to the local drugstore and sat at the soda fountain to catch up on one another's lives. As she sipped her Green River and her friend drank her cherry coke, she was told "how fortunate" she was. Shirley agreed, yet, there was this one thing, she started to say, but then halted. Her friend urged her on, "What one thing, what is it?" "Well, we are staying with my parents, in their small apartment, and life would be perfect if we could be on our own. I just am not sure we can afford some of the high rents around here." Leaning on the counter, her friend asked: "Is your husband, Bud, is it? Is he an ex-serviceman?" Wondering what that had to do with housing, Shirley told of Bud's time in the Air Corps during the war. Grinning, her friend said: "Well, for heaven's sake girl, you guys could live in government housing! That's what it's for, y'know?!" "What is that—government housing? Where is it, I mean how do you get in?" "Well, there are many places in Illinois, here in Chicago there are several, that's where my husband and I live, down Fullerton Avenue, near Central! It's really great, everyone knows everyone and helps one another out, because they are all ex-service people!" As Shirley walked to her parents afterward, she was finding it hard to keep from singing out loud, but she knew she had promised to keep things to herself, and intended to do that, for now. The next day she began making telephone calls, and within a couple of hours, after many tries, she had set up an appointment for she and Bud, the following weekend. He had only to bring his discharge papers, and they would need their marriage certificate. When Bud was told of the appointment she had arranged, he was not as eager as she was, but she would not back down on this one. Nosiree! Without mentioning their destination to her parents they headed for the office she had been given directions for, and there, they were treated with such respect, Shirley was feeling very confident. Soon they were told there was an opening for them in one of the larger trailers, located on the outskirts of the city. They drove over there that same afternoon to see what it was like. Driving to the end of the Kedzie avenue line, there was the huge expanse before them. Getting out of their vehicle they walked slowly down the sidewalk, seeking the office, and soon found it. The gentleman there, took the paper from Bud's hand and walked them to the far end of the area. Then they walked past a large, expandable trailer on the corner, for large families it was explained. Across the sidewalk from it, was the laundry room, with washing machines and dryers! (Her parents always sent the laundry out each week, or mother washed things by hand, on a scrubbing board in the tub, wouldn't this be something, Shirley mused washing machines and dryer's?!) The three continued down the walk, passing two trailers, and at last came to the one on the end, which they were told, was theirs, if they wanted it. "If we want it?", thought Shirley, "Oh yeah, we sure do want it!" Leaving them on their own he handed over the key and suggested they look around. Once inside, it was larger than it had seemed at first sight. There was a room as you came in the door, with a couch across the back wall, which opened into a full bed. There was a kitchen area, with a double hotplate and sink, and much cabinet space, below and above and across from that was closet space and more shelves for linens. The back half would accommodate a crib, dresser and more! It looked wonderful to Shirley's wondering eyes, and it would be theirs alone! A place to raise their baby, with no interference, oh joy! Bud turned to look at her, and started to laugh, he said: "I was going to ask 'what do you thin?', but just looking at you, I already know the answer, you love it, don't you?!" "I do, I really do, but is this too far for you to drive to work? It's a good half hour or more from my parents, will it be alright?" "Remember, I drive all day, I will just put in for a change of route and it will be perfectly fine. The people at 7UP are very family conscious so if you like it, I think we should go back to the office and find out how much this is going to cost, because before long you won't be working and we will be living on my paycheck only." That brought Shirley down to earth in a hurry, she had no idea of the cost, just that her friend said it was 'reasonable' but what exactly, was reasonable she worried as they walked toward the office. The man looked up from his desk and smiled at them: "Well, what do you think?", he asked. Bud took charge, steering Shirley into the chair across the desk then turning he asked what the rent would be, would it be paid by the week or month, did it include heating (he'd noticed there was a furnace set into the side wall). Laughing, holding his hand before his face, as though to ward off a blow, he responded with a "Whoa there, one question at a time, I'm only a lowly clerk you know!" They looked at him questioningly, and he hastened to add that he had noted Bud had been in the Air Corps as he had been and he was letting him know that he was out-ranked. That relaxed Bud instantly, he laughed too, "Sorry, he said, but my wife has done most of the work getting us here, and I am not familiar how this works." Shirley glowed with pleasure at being praised for her efforts. Such a unique experience for her! So, together they listened as they discovered a whole new world before them. The electricity was included as was the water, however they would have to pay for their own fuel, which wouldn't be too much, he allowed, as the place was well insulated. As for the rent, it is due every month, they would receive a notice with a self-addressed envelope a week before it was due. The trailer theyhad been allotted was $25.00 a month! They both gasped, that was the same amount they had been paying her mother! They quickly signed the papers, went back and checked the trailer out to see what they would need to set up housekeeping. They'd been told that the people before them had left the couch and they could either keep it, or throw it out, it was their choice. They examined it thoroughly and felt it clean and in good enough shape to keep. All the way home Shirley could not stop talking, so excited was she, and finally Bud got caught up too. They were like little children planning what they would do, what they would put where, what a dream come true this was. Shirley felt she would probably be thanking God the rest of the night, so grateful was she at this turn of events. Surprisingly her parents didn't put up an argument, not that it would have done any good, Shirley thought to herself, yet she was relieved that everything would work out without any further discord. Same was true of Bud's parents, they seemed please to know "the kid's" were going to be in their own place.

Once she was into her third month, before she began to 'show', Shirley had gone to her boss, and privately told him of her condition. To work in an office, while pregnant was not acceptable, and so they agreed on the date she would leave. He suggested she simply take a leave of absence, so she could return after the baby was born. Sadly, she shook her head, "No", she said, "I want to stay home with my baby, I won't be returning, I'm sorry—but I will train whomever you hire to take my place, I promise." He smiled in appreciation, but stated she had done everything that had needed to get set up, and it would be easy for someone to do the job she had created, by simply following her directions. Reluctantly, he wished her luck in her new life, and she smiled, thinking: "Ah, here I thought I didn't have a new life, ah, but now, I do!!" She stayed until September and then left for good, from her job, her friends, and onto the future.

By this time, they had moved their belongings into the trailer that they had cleaned and painted with fresh paint. The cabinets were all stained and had simply to be cleaned and polished to look like new. The sink and hotplates were all clean the people before them had obviously been good housekeepers. The shower gifts they had received had included towel sets, and sheets, so t hey hadn't needed to buy any. They got lamps that hung on the walls for lighting and they had a table that folded down at night, but was big enough for four to eat around, and their chairs folded as well. It amazed Bud that Shirley could be so innovative, he had no idea how thrilled she was to create a real home for them. As she began to gain weight, she had told Bud she was 'getting fat' and he took her in his arms, and said she was not getting fat, she was getting more beautiful! This man fed her ego, and she really began to believe that maybe she wasn't as bad as she'd always been told, nor as stupid either. Once settled in, their next door neighbors came over and introduced themselves as The Hunts. He was Chester and she was June. The were older than Bud and Shirley, by some eight years, but were so friendly that soon they became a foursome, often having dinner at one another's trailers, and playing cards afterward. When winter came the trailer remained warm and cozy just as predicted, and once again, she thought life was good, almost too good.

In January, she began suffering with a terrible backache, not realizing this was a form of labor, they nearly didn't make it to the hospital on time. As it was, Bud had suggested she spend the day with her mother so if she needed anything her mother could see to it. He was going to work, planning to pick her up afterward, when the pains became even more fierce, her worried mother phoned the neighbor across the street who was a nurse and asked if she could come by. As soon as she saw Shirley she knew she was in labor and needed to get to the hospital, quickly. Of course, Shirley didn't want to go without Bud, but there was no way to reach him. Rose called the elderly landlord who lived in the apartment below, and he said he would drive them to the Hospital, which wasn't very far away. Bundling up against the terrible cold and fierce January winds they made it to his car. Soon they were driving, slowly due to the icy conditions and Shirley, frantic now, worried that the baby would come before Bud could make it. When they pulled up in front of the hospital, she looked out the window in dismay! It was the wrong hospital! He had driven them to St. Mary's and she was expected at St. Elizabeth's where hopefully her doctor was waiting. Once again, they were driving through the stormy day, and it was with immense relief that they made it to the right hospital. The nurse put Shirley into a wheelchair and wheeled her away as her mother went to sign her in. Somehow, in the confusion, her mother had said 'Sister' to the nun at the desk, and it was noted that she was Shirley's sister, and thus they would not let her up to be with her daughter. In the throes of childbirth, left on her own, Shirley was more frightened than she ever had been. At last her doctor appeared and told her it would be awhile yet, but 'everything was going well'. True to his word, he helped her deliver an 8 pound 6½ ounce baby boy that night of the 16th. Nine days later she was released and able to go home. Shirley so loved being a mother, and although she was unable to nurse her firstborn, she took great joy in his health and in caring for him. He was to be named John, Shirley's favorite name, with Michael as his middle name. Then came the problem with religion that was not supposed to occur! Of course, Shirley wanted her son to be baptized, but Bud refused to sign the papers presented to him by the priest, so it never happened. Because she didn't drive, her church attendance had fallen aside as well. So although she was free of her parents, and had a home of her own, she was dependent on Bud to drive her anywhere. About this time he came home to tell her of what he thought to be a most exciting bit of information! It seemed he had met an old high school friend who was in the construction business, and who made a great salary. He planned to leave his truck driving job and become a tuck pointer! Yes, he supposed, it was dangerous, but the money would make it worthwhile. It was fortunate that Shirley was happy to play the role of wife and mother, as there wasn't much else for her to do. When Bud got paid on Friday, he would stop and cash his check and "have a few beers with the guys", and she saw no harm in that. He would hand over money for her to shop with, and the only bills they had were the rent and telephone. It never entered her mind to ask how much he actually earned, in her parents home it was made clear that her father's wages were not any of her business. After all, she was only 19, a young mother quite pleased with her life, who would put her baby into the buggy and walk around the area during the day. She felt life was good, although Bud came home at different times, and it could be difficult to gauge dinnertime, it all worked out well, as there were only the two of them, the baby being on his own schedule. Some nights he'd come home obviously bordering on being drunk, but when questioned there would always be a story that ended up with "the guys" being at fault. He never missed a day of work, was up and gone by 6 a.m. so how could she complain? He never required breakfast, he and "the guys" always stopped for coffee and donuts, so she slept in until the baby needed feeding. Often the neighbors would sit out on the doorsteps of their trailer, with everyone singing the recent songs of the time. In short it was a good life, until one warm June night she began to feel ill, and sick to her stomach. Blaming the heat, she went into their trailer early that night. Then her neighbor friend asked her the following morning if she was feeling any better. Shirley told her she was surprised the beat was bothering her so, never had before, and her friend said maybe the heat is bothering you, because you're pregnant! Shockwaves went through her as she checked her calendar. First she was devastated, could they afford another baby? Not knowing what their financial status was, she knew she best sound out Bud before telling him of her fears. The following Saturday morning she questioned him had he ever thought of having another baby? He looked at her for a few minutes, rather narrow-eyed, and said flatly: "You're not pregnant, are you?" Tearfully, she looked up at him and slowly nodded, waiting for the slap to the head. Instead he leaned back smiling and said: "Well, I really am some kind of man, ain't I tho?" Shirley breathed a sigh of relief as he headed for the tavern across the way, but she felt frightened as well. When waiting for Johnny to be born, she had been given something called "twilight sleep' to relax her, plus a few drops of ether on her face mask throughout the birthing process, then as they stitched her up she was given a few whiffs of gas! Sick?! She had felt so sick, she thought she wouldn't make it through it. Of course she was kept in bed for 8 days and on the final 9th day was allowed to 'dangle her feet'! She had been so weakened it had frightened her, and the thought of going through this again, wasn't something she cared to think about. They had been practicing what the doctor had referred to as "the rhythm system" a form of birth control, condoned by the Church. Well, obviously it hadn't worked for them! Yet as the days passed she began to think how nice it would be for Johnny to have a brother or sister only 14 months younger than him! How great that could be. Plus once the first couple of days of morning sickness passed she once again enjoyed good health, so she began to relax. When her next door neighbor asked how she was feeling, Shirley smiled her happiness. Joining together for a cup of coffee at one point she asked who her doctor was. Hesitating, Shirley confessed she had not been to a doctor, since she had moved here her doctor was too far away. Well, she was informed she must see a doctor, it was unacceptable to have no pre-natal care! She had three children of her own, and made regular visits to the nearby county clinic with them and said she would be happy to bring Shirley as well. Even though Bud had assured her that giving birth is 'a natural' thing, it was explained to her at the clinic pregnancy doesn't really take care of itself. They gave her vitamins, and iron pills, monitored her weight as well as her over-all health. In her final month she was given the name of the hospital she would go to, and that the amount would be $85.00 to be paid in full, before her entering. The money was put aside and by the first week in

April, on a beautiful sunny morning her second son, James entered this world at 8 pounds, 11 ounces! He was born by natural methods, with no drugs administered, and Shirley watched his arrival through a large mirror. Six hours later she stood at the window, viewing the new grass, and budding flowers, marveling how 'easy' childbirth could be! Three days later, thanking God over and over, she arrived back home to a waiting Johnny, anxious to meet his new little brother, Jimmy. One of the first things she did was to thank her friend, next door, for having seen to it she attended the clinic. Through their help she learned much to see herself and her family through the many rough years to come.

That Thanksgiving they were invited to her in-laws for dinner, living in the trailer with a 2-burner hotplate she made simple meals. There was an oven-type attachment so she could make small roasts, but certainly not a turkey, so they looked forward to the day. Her father-in-law had obviously been drinking earlier and the wine at dinner had a quick effect on him. He began dropping his silver and had food dribbling down his chin. Bud's mother began her deriding words, encouraging Bud to join in. Shirley nudged Bud, whispering he is your father, after all. Then wakened by the loud voices Johnny started crying, running to the bedroom Shirley was kept as Jimmy joined in. Once baby had gone back to sleep, she closed the door and came out carrying Johnny, only to witness a most terrifying scene. There was Bud, standing over his father with both fists pounding into his head! The blood was literally pouring down his forehead, into his eyes. She stood there, hugging her son to her, in shock! She heard this voice saying, "Again . . . hit him again, Bud!" There was her mother-in-law, her eyes glazed as though she were in a hypnotic trance, repeating the same words. She let out a shrill "Nooo", when frightened Johnny began to howl, and twist and turn in her arms, she tried to gain control. Her sounds had reached Bud, though, and as he looked at her he began to slowly stand up to his full height. He stared down at his father, looked up at his mother in such a dazed way, as though wondering what had happened! She went to him, took him in her arms, patting his back and saying, "It's alright, baby . . . it's all right!" Shocked, Shirley couldn't believe her eyes or her ears! Her husband, beaten bloody, semi-conscious ignored while she consoled her son! Suddenly ill, Shirley ran to the bathroom, gently laying Johnny on the bathmat, she hung her head over the toilet retching. Splashing cold water on her face, she retrieved her baby and returned to the living room to find her mother-in-law bathing her husbands' face. She was murmuring to him as though he were a child, meanwhile Bud leaned against the front door, quite obviously shaken, with a cigarette in one hand and a can of beer in the other. Looking up at him, Shirley said, "I want to leave now." He nodded his head, shamefully, and took Johnny in his arms as Shirley got little Jimmy and they left. The feelings of revulsion never left Shirley's memories.

After that episode she avoided contact with her in-laws as much as possible. She began to feel that "must get away feeling" once again, and began seeking new housing through the government. She had found work a few months after Jimmy's birth, as a tuck pointer bud would not work once the first frost came, and would be off until the Spring thaw which could be into March. During her walks around the area with her two boys in the buggy she had seen a "Waitress wanted" sign in the local restaurant. She mentioned it to Bud and he watched the boys as she went to seek employment. Never having been a waitress she didn't know what to say, but fortunately for her, the head waitress interviewed her in the owners absence. When she was asked how much experience she had she was truthful, saying she had none. The Waitress looked at her aghast! "Don't tell Sydney that when you come in tomorrow. Just tell him you worked in several places, in another state! Don't worry, I'll cover for you", she said with her hand up to prevent Shirley from saying anything further. "Trust me on this, I'll show you the ropes!" Next morning Shirley met with the owner and tried to bluff him, as she'd been told to do, but Sydney didn't look as though he believed her. Thinking quickly, Shirley added: "But-I'll work FREE, just keep my tips, for a week, then if you don't want to hire me, I'll leave." "FREE?! You'll work for no wages for a week?" he repeated. Nodding, Shirley looked him in the eye, and he graced her with a huge smile! "You're hired!" he said. Shirley worked hard, but found she really enjoyed the time being with people once again. Being a stay at home mom had been wonderful, and she would still be able to do that, while she worked nights Bud would be with the boys. They were contacted by the government that they would be getting a change in housing the following spring. Perfect! Bud would be back to work, they would have a larger place, meanwhile her tips were very generous!

That August Shirley gave birth to a darling little baby girl! Bud wanted to call her Joyce and so she was named: Joyce Marie. They were located a good distance from the city of Chicago now, away from both his parents and hers, and although Bud continued to drink too much, it didn't seem to matter anymore. Shirley had a cute little place to live in and decorate. There were three bedrooms, however she chose to put all three cribs into the largest one. She painted each wall, from floor to ceiling with cartoonish like animals! On one wall was a squirrel sitting on a tree stump, with acorns all around in the grass. On the other wall was a bunny rabbit sitting amid all colors of flowers, the third wall had a huge purple cow, with yellow spots and a most contented face! A huge window took up the fourth wall, which looked onto a sizable yard, with a forest preserve beyond the fence.

Things were good once again, Bud was back to work, she was at peace. They were even able to have their first television, which in 1950, was of course, black and white. However, it was amazing to have these images portraying other worlds, right there in your own living room! Bud still worked in the city so kept touch with his mother by stopping before coming home which was fine with Shirley. One August night shortly after Joyce was born, they received a phone call that bud's father was dying. He'd gone to the doctor for a checkup and was told he should be hospitalized. He was in a Veterans' Hospital, which was the place Shirley saw him for the last time. He was deathly pale, with tubes running through him in all directions. he reached out to Shirley and took her hand, and winked at her. Slowly he closed his eyes but before he did he looked right at Shirley once again and nodded his head. She stood over him, asking if there was anything she could do. She told the nurse she felt he was trying to say something, but was told she couldn't remove the tubing. She suggested Shirley put her ear close to his mouth, she did. He whispered: "I'm dying . . . it's alright . . . you are a good girl . . . don't . . . . don't . . ." then he was gone. "Don't what?" she wondered. Don't worry? Don't stay? (with Bud?) She would never know.

Then in 1952, after her second daughter, Judy May was born in July, death came again. Bud was late in coming home, which in itself was not too unusual, but what was odd, was that he was in his bosses vehicle, instead of their car. He dashed into the house and said Shirley should get the next door neighbor to watch the kid's as her father was dying-in the hospital! Seemed that rather than going back to the office to retrieve his car after work he and 'the guys' had gone for a few drinks so he didn't get the message her mother had left there. Now he'd taken ½ and hour to drive home and then another ½ hour to get to the hospital! Shirley felt angry and shocked that her mother hadn't tried to call her directly, rather than through Bud's work. Even though they had no telephone of their own, the next door neighbor had given permission for them to receive any calls and her mother had that number! When they arrived at the hospital where she had given birth to Judy, 5 months earlier, she dashed into the lobby. By time she had the room number, and was waiting for the elevator Bud came in to stand beside her. It seemed to Shirley to crawl up the four floors, and slowly open its doors. She stepped into the hallway glancing around, taking in the room numbers, just then a door down the hall opened, drawing her attention. As she watched, her mother came out of the room, her head down. Shirley hurried to her. "Mother?" she asked. Her mother seemed surprised to see her, then after a few seconds she said: "Oh, it's you . . . you're too late. He's dead. It's just as well, though, he looked terrible with all those tubes . . . just as well you're late." She wasn't crying. She just stood there, with a resigned look, subdued, quiet. Shirley reached out to her, asking if she was alright? Looking rather surprised Rose said: "Yes, I'm all right, but I would appreciate a ride home, I came her in a police car." Shirley asked what on earth had happened? She couldn't seem to take it in. Her mother said: "Well, your father left the house for work this morning, same as usual, at 7:30. At about 8:15 the police came to the house to notify me that my husband had been found on the sidewalk, about three blocks from home, unconscious. He had been taken to the hospital and in looking through his wallet it showed his identification, rather than telephone such news, they came in person and brought me to the hospital." She had been there ever since. He would regain consciousness now and again, but never realized where he was or who she was, or indeed what was happening. As she began to tell of his loss of bodily function control the tears began to come. She wept silently the rest of the way home. When they got her upstairs they sat at the kitchen table while she went to change her clothes, and they quietly spoke of how Shirley could stay the night while Bud would go home and pick up the children to bring them the next morning. Her head swimming, Shirley couldn't get past the thought that her mother had known of this since 8 a.m. and had never made the effort to reach her, still this was no time to comment. Soon Rose reappeared and with a smile said she was going to put on a pot of coffee, because her two friends should be arriving soon. Shirley said: "Friends? What friends?" Rose then informed them she had called Neddie and Edna before her husband had died and they were coming to spend the night with her and help her with the funeral arrangements the next morning. Shirley, looked at her in amazement, saying: "Mother, I was going to stay with you—" At which, Rose looked at her and said: "You? Why would I want YOU here? You go home with Bud, where you belong, take care of your kids, I'll take care of things here!" Bud smiled at Shirley, obviously relieved he would have to do no more. "See? It's all taken care of, we'll come back for the funeral." Still, Shirley sat thinking it was after all, her father and she owned him respect, if nothing else. Even though she had just been told how little she was needed she felt she should be there for support. What a laugh that turned out to be, for as those thoughts tumbled through her mind within a space of a few seconds time, things changed quite abruptly! As her friends walked in with their arms outstretched Rose was up in a flash, running to them, burying herself in one after the others ample bosoms! Playing the role of bereaved widow to the hilt! Soon her friends had her seated, putting a coffee cup in her hands, hovering over her, and she seemed to be reveling in the attention. Soon she told Shirley to go home, it was really late! Both friends looked up and agreed that they would take care of Rose and all the arrangements. The end result, of course, was that they did leave. On telephoning the next day she was advised that her mother "was resting" and couldn't come to the phone now, but everything was under control. Then, somewhat as an afterthought she was advised her fathers' funeral would be on January 16th (Johnny's third birthday)! Feeling as though she had been edged out of her mother's life, and the fact that she'd not been contacted to have at least seen her father before he breathed his last, Shirley resigned herself, as she always had.

For about a year things went on fairly well. Living a distance away from his mother made life easier for Shirley. She had purchased a new car, and was enjoying her independence, how often Bud was with her she neither knew nor cared. As for her mother, she heard little from her either.

About a year after her fathers death Bud came home in a really drunken state. He was in an angry mood and, of course, the most logical one to reap the anger was Shirley. It was stormy all day and having no way to get to the local grocer except by walking, with all four youngsters, Shirley decided to make do with what she had to prepare supper. She had made spaghetti sauce but having no spaghetti noodles used another type of pasta. By time he arrived the children were all fed and in bed. When one works as a construction worker and it rains all day, the most logical solution was for them to hang out in a tavern, playing pool and drinking. When he came in the door, Shirley knew she would have to be careful what she said, it was obvious he was in bad shape. When he growled: "What's for supper?" She hurried to get his plate set down before him. Without any warning all hell broke loose! He screamed and ranted that he worked hard and all he expected when he came home as a decent dinner. And what was this mess, anyway?! Before she realized what was to come he threw the dishful of food across the room, where spaghetti sauce began to run down the wall. As she went to clean up he was suddenly behind her, quick as a tiger, he took the pot full of leftovers and deliberately dumped them across the kitchen floor! Stunned into silence, Shirley stood and looked at the awful mess, thinking how tired she was and how it would take hours to clean up the mess he had created. Then she did what infuriated him more than anything . . . she began to cry! It all seemed so hopeless. There she was, stooped over, cleaning the floor, tears running down, seeing everything thru a blur. When suddenly there was an explosion in her head! She blinked, shook her head and looked around, to find herself sitting on the floor. The pan she had been putting the spilled food into was still in her hand, unfortunately it was overturned and filled her lap. Still with blurred vision, she looked across the room to see Bud had removed one heavy work shoe and was in the process of removing the other. As she looked down on the floor next to her she saw the other shoe and realized she had been struck in the head with it! No wonder she was stunned and hurting. Even as she put this thought together he threw the second shoe, and there was no time to do more than duck, which she did. As she looked around her two arms which she had instinctively locked overhead for protection, she saw Bud coming toward her. Later, she only remembered screaming: "No No" . . . she felt the first few blows, but then didn't recall much else. When next she became aware, she was sprawled across the kitchen floor, hurting, she tired to get up. She heard the television and managed to crawl to the living room doorway and look in. She saw Bud asleep, or more likely passed out, sitting in the chair. Cautiously she crept to the children's bedroom, and they were all sound asleep! Quickly throwing her raincoat over her shoulders she went to the next door neighbor and asked to use her telephone. She looked at Shirley in shock! Later, Shirley realized she must have been quite a sight to behold-face beaten and bruised, hair disheveled and covered from head to toe with spaghetti sauce! Her neighbor never really gave permission, just backed away allowing her to enter, and stood there staring as Shirley called the police. For the first time in her married life Shirley was reaching out for help. The man on the phone told her to go back home quietly and not to wake Bud, that there would be officers there shortly. Shaking violently, she returned home, checked once again to see if Bud was still out, he was, and she sat at the kitchen table, waiting for the squad . . . and her salvation. As she sat there, she knew Bud would be livid when he found out what she'd one, but she was afraid, he had nearly killed her this time, and someone, somewhere had to take her side. Soon the squad pulled up, no siren, no lights, she noted gratefully. She opened the door and they came in. They stood staring at her, then slowly taking in the entire kitchen covered with sauce, she knew how she must look but for the first time she wasn't embarrassed. She knew deep inside her this was not her fault. They asked: "Where is he?" She pointed toward the living room. The other officer sat across from her and asked her what had happened—from the beginning—he said. So she told him. He asked if this sort of thing had happened before, and was told yes, the beatings, yes, but this was the worst yet, plus four children were sleeping in the next room! He then asked if she would be willing to sign a complaint against Bud. Shirley asked what exactly that meant, and was told if she would sign they would arrest him, it would go to court and the judge would make the final decision as to disposition. Shirley really didn't understand what that meant! However she did understand what going to jail might mean. She was fearful of such a mar on Bud's record, would he lose his job? Tearfully she asked the officer if there wasn't some way that he and his partner could just threaten Bud that he was never to hit her again—or else? She was reluctant to sign any paper called a complaint or anything else. Today, with changes in the law, I suppose this sounds strange, but there she was, 23 years old, with four children! How could she take care of them if Bud was in jail? Plus she was living in Veterans housing, would she be able to remain here? All these thoughts literally flew through her head, as the officer sat facing her, she wondered if, after all there was any hope for her?! Soon the other officer appeared with Bud in tow. Shirley held her breath, and with all the strength she could muster, looked up at him. She knew in her heart of hearts she wanted him to reach out to her . . . to say he was sorry, to say it would never happen again. Now that he knew she had been smart/brave enough to at last call for outside help, now maybe they could start a new and better life. But when their eyes met it was enough to make her trembling begin all over again. There was such violence pouring out of his eyes Shirley had to avert her own. The officer had him by the arm and said over his shoulder, to Shirley: "Well, lady, are you willing to sign a complaint—or not?" Shirley winced, looked at bud once again, still there was this venom pouring from his eyes and she made the decision then and there, knowing full well if she allowed those policemen to leave without him, he'd continue the beating until . . . until what? She filled her lungs with air and breathed out a: "Yes, I'll sign." The officer took out a pad and began to write while the other told Bud to get his shoes on and a coat, he was going for a ride!

As he began to obey Shirley saw his shocked and unbelieving eyes search to make contact with her, but she avoided his gaze this time. Fifteen minutes later she still sat at the table, in the silent house. Finally, reaching deep inside she found the inner strength to begin to clean up the now-dried disgusting mess. As she moved, painfully, the kitchen slowly got back in order. When at last, she was able to stand in the warm, soothing water of the shower she began to realize how good it felt to be clean. Slipping on a clean nightly she once again checked the locks on the door and sunk into her bed in relief. The next morning when she awoke and began getting the children's breakfast ready she was glad she had taken the time to clean the kitchen the night before, because her head hurt so bad she didn't know if she could bend to do it then. Looking in the mirror she was shocked at the bruised and battered face that she saw reflected. Tentatively she touched the top of her head which was so tender where the heavy shoe had struck her. Still aspirin and love for her children got her through the morning. Then, shortly before noon, Shirley was shocked to see her mother-in-laws car pull up. She couldn't believe it, she thought to herself that woman would never take a day off work, why was she here? As she looked through the kitchen curtains she suddenly, frighteningly knew why!

There he was, Bud! Calmly climbing out of the passengers side. She was so scared, she didn't know what to do! She began to tremble, standing there frozen. They got to the locked door and stood looking ahead should she open it? The boys were playing in the living room and both girls were down for a nap. She looked toward the children, then back to the window, where she met Bud's eyes staring at her. Dropping the curtain she began to breathe hard. Then they knocked on the door, and trance-like she opened it. Then she backed away into the living room as they entered. Bud came toward her, reaching out to take her arms, ever so gently, in his hands. As she flinched at the contact, he stood looking down at her, saying over and over how sorry he was, how it would never happen again. Finally, she realized he was talking—no begging her—to forgive him. Meanwhile the children's full attention was centered on Grandma who had come laden with gifts for them. During the time after he had been taken away Shirley had convinced herself that she would never be able to support herself, let alone four little ones, still, he had shown no remorse last night she remembered. Speechless, she stood looking form him to his mother, what had brought about this change? Then it came—loud and clear—! His mother pushed him aside, gently, of course, then turned to put her arms around Shirley. "Honey", she said, "I know this has been hard on you, but you both know you can't go out and work and make enough money to take care of these kids. Now you and Bud have to sit down and talk out your problems. Everything is going to be fine, just you wait and see. Why, I've got a nice little surprise for you. I'll pay for all this trouble you have caused, and we will all forget it ever happened. You should have known better than to call the police, and give our Buddy a police record, that was a terribly cruel thing to do, but we'll forgive you for acting foolishly and now that I'm h ere and see your 'new' place, I'm sure I'll find lots of nice things I can buy you to make it even better. You'll see, everything will be just fine. Bud get the things out of the car so we can have lunch." He went out to the car, and returned with sandwich makings, and a stunned Shirley watched as lunch as prepared.

On Court Day her mother-in-law not only accompanied them, but drove them to Court. All the way there she spoke to Shirley as though she were of the age of the children she had left in the neighbors' care. In a quiet, soothing voice she kept "explaining" how they would both forgive and forget Shirley's trespasses! Things were going to be just fine from now on, if she would just remember to tell the Judge how 'over-excited' she was when she had called the police after what was a small family tiff. "Tiff?", thought Shirley . . . "Tiff?!" Her pain continued to be felt, bruises were still visible. Her head had an egg on it, which she was certainly aware of when she tired to brush her hair! Still, she sat listening, unable to speak, still traumatized. Seated in the courtroom, Shirley tired to become invisible, she was so in awe of all that was happening around her. Then she and Bud were called up before the Judge and Gladys joined them! She was half out of her mind with fright, having just witnessed several cases where people were sentenced to jail terms. Seeing this God-like man before her, in his impressive black robe was almost more than she could bear. As he leaned forward, eh looked first down at her, then at Bud, then she saw his eyebrows arch in a frown as he looked at Gladys. He asked who she was and why was she standing before him when only two people had been called. Of course, she was delighted to have this opportunity and she took another step toward the Bench. Immediately she said: "Your Honor, this is my son and his wife—" That was as far as she got, he interrupted her saying: "Fine, suppose you just stay there (pointing at the floor) and remain silent, or I will have you removed from my courtroom! Do you understand?" Shirley was stunned! No one could tell Gladys to be silent, but this man sure did! She glanced sideways to see Gladys take a respectful step backward with a shocked look on her face. Nervous as she was, it was all Shirley could do to refrain from laughing aloud. Next the Judge turned his attention to Bud, asking: 'Are you the husband?" When Bud nodded (probably as shocked as Shirley had been at hearing his mother rebuked) yes. The Judge spoke loudly for all to hear, as he said: "Young man, when I speak to you I expect a verbal response, do you understand me?!" A surprised Bud stammered: "Yes sir!" The judge corrected him and said firmly: "Yes, Your Honor!" "Yes, Your Honor", Bud repeated quickly. Leaning toward Bud once again, the judge asked how old he was, and when Bud stated he was 26, he added: "Your Honor" without any prompting, Shirley noticed. These last few exchanges had quite an affect on her, she began to feel hope that maybe calling the Police had not been as foolish as she had been led to believe. Focusing on the exchange she heard the Judge continue his comments. He said: "I see you are quite a tall, well-built young man, were you in the Armed Services?" Bud responded that he had been in the Army Air Corps, and added he had a honorable discharge. Leaning back some, the Judge placed both hands in front of him, and responded: "I see, and what do you do for a living now?" Rather proudly, Bud answered: "I am a tuck pointer, Your Honor." The Judge looked up and said: "Hmm, that is physical type work isn't it? Keeps you strong—in shape?" Stumbling in confusion, Bud replied that yes, he supposed so. Then the Judge turned to Shirley, and asked how old she was. Shirley replied: "23, Your Honor." though it took a few tries to get past the lump she had developed in her throat! In a gentle voice he asked her how many children she had, and she responded: "four—2 boys and 2 girls, Your Honor." Then he asked their ages and she recited: "4, 3, 2 years and a baby, 3 months", then remembering, added: "Your Honor." Because they were in her realm of expertise, she began to relax. Then another strange question was asked of her, "How tall are you?" When she answered that she was 4'11", she watched as the Judge looked from her to Bud, she had lost some of her earlier fear as she sensed a caring, kindness coming from him as he looked her in the eye. However, when he turned back to look at Bud, she saw his intense blue eyes become steely as they pierced into Bud! Then in a forceful voice he thundered: "How could an admittedly strong man, such as yourself use physical force on such a little person as she?! She has given you four children to raise and father, what possible excuse can you give me for such violence?" It seemed Bud looked as though he might answer, when the Judge held up his hand, and said: "Don't bother to answer, because we both know, there is no answer. No excuse. Do you understand? There is no rhyme nor reason for a husband to physically abuse his wife as you have done this past week, and as I understand other times in the past. No man h as a right to lay a hand in force on his wife, a marriage license is not a license to beat another human being into subjection! A marriage license should be proof of two people seeking the same things, through love. It is a binding contract of love and caring, not force, do you hear what I am saying to you?" As Bud stood, head dejectedly down, suddenly another voice was heard! Gladys stepped forward, once again, and spoke up loudly, "Your Honor", she said, "These two do have a good marriage. It's just that with four children there is so much pressure on my son to support the family that it is understandable that he would expect a decent meal, not some thrown together jumble. Shirley may be young but she has her duties to perform as a housewife too—and her first allegiance should be to her husband after all." Shirley turned, open-mouthed to stare at her! This remark from a woman who had urged her son to beat her own husband, at least one time

Shirley knew of. Still, she didn't speak up in her own defense, knowing Bud had not come home from a hard days work, but from a hard days drinking! No, she thought, I can't help but admit I should have had a better dinner, but I did the best I was able to—

Then, her thoughts were interrupted by the Judge who in an angry tone, with those steely eyes flashing, began to use his gavel as he stared at Gladys. Then, very quietly, he spoke: "Ma'am, did I not tell you to stand in place and remain silent?" Not waiting for her to reply he continued, "I might well hold you in contempt of this court!" As she opened her mouth to speak, he again held up that hand, signaling silence, as she had earlier done to Bud. Then he want on to say: "This man is your son, which gave you the responsibility of teaching him proper behavior. You seem to have been remiss in this area. As I have told him, and repeat to you: 'No human being has the right to inflict personal injury on another', and if you feel his behavior was acceptable, you, madam, need counseling. If the world were run by the stronger always taking from the weaker this world would soon die off, quite rightly so, I might add. If you stand here in concern for your grandchildren, and for these young people having a future life together, I would suggest you allow them to build a strong marriage, not dependent on brute force. Do I make myself clear? Freeing your son by paying his bail, was not a smart move in that direction. Now, I will not hold you in contempt at this time, but would be remiss if I didn't warn you to be more cautious in your behavior in the future. Now, please be seated." This being said, he then turned to Shirley, whose head was swimming, she could not believe the concern he had showed for her and her children. She found tears were sliding down her cheeks, in gratitude. She thought maybe, just maybe, people like this judge, might actually reach out and help her make it on her own. But then, reality came right on the heels of those thoughts. She had worked as a waitress, yes, but only when Bud was not working and could stay with the children. All the old fears of losing her babies formed a knot in her stomach, and she knew she needed to remain married, no matter the consequences. She looked into the judges eyes as he encouraged her to speak up, tell the whole truth as to what happened that night. She tried to concentrate on the things he was saying to her. She realized he wanted her to stand up for herself, tell the truth. Press charges, have Bud jailed, for as long as the Judge deemed necessary. She licked her dry lips, pulled her eyes from his, and hoarsely whispered she would not press charges. She tearfully said she was sure this would never happen again, they needed to work harder at their marriage, for their children as well as themselves. She risked a quick look at the Judge to see disappointment, yet understanding too. He seemed to know she was frightened of not being able to care for those four little ones, and had probably known all along this would be the end result, yet he had taken advantage of the opportunity to read off both Bud and his mother, in front of her, hoping it might do some good. What he did not know was that the force they used on her was not physical force that made her back down, but the threat of taking her children away! On the return drive home she was advised by her mother-in-law that she should be thoroughly ashamed for airing their dirty laundry in such a public way! She should also be aware that she had caused both her and Bud to miss these days of work, but before she could add anything further Bud turned to her with two words: "Enough, Mother!" No more was said after that, she simply dropped them off and drove away. Once the children were back home again, Shirley and Bud tried hard to make the rest of their day pleasant as possible. For a time, things did get better, Bud seemed to be making an effort. He would get home as early as 6 p.m. and many evenings they would have dinner together as a family, once the two little girls were sleeping for the night. Shirley began to relax, thinking that she had done the right thing after all, regardless of what her mother-in-law had said. Perhaps that Judge really had gotten through to him she thought. Life could be good for their little family. He even seemed to enjoy playing with the boys, and displayed real affection for their oldest daughter. She was so little, so petite, with blonde curly hair and a sweet smile. Soon Halloween came and the boys were so excited at the prospect of going out and "twicks and tweating', but of course there was no extra money for costumes, or a sewing machine to create them! Somehow Shirley managed to create two costumes out of old curtain scraps, from when they'd lived in the trailer! They were thrilled to go happily from door to door with their little faces made up from lipstick and eyebrow pencil, two of the most adorable little 'old ladies' you ever saw! Bud was late coming home that night, so she got the boys washed up, and with rosy cheeks and shiny eyes they happily went to bed, leaving their bags of 'tweets' on the table for Daddy to see. When Bud got home, Shirley saw with that old remembered sinking feeling, he was drunk. He lurched over to the stove and slurred: "I didn't wanna' eat your garbage so I had a decent meal at mother's. She nodded in agreement, and put the left-overs into their old Shelvador. She went into the living room to wait him out, thinking when he fell asleep she could get into bed and he'd never waken. She sat on the couch, with the television on low, when suddenly he came into the room and stood between her and the screen. He forced these encounters and she had no idea of what was coming. Having had these past months of reprieve she was out of practice as to how to handle them. Finally she looked up at him, and asked what was wrong! He pulled his arms out from behind his back and she saw he had the boy's tricks or treat bags, one in each hand. "What is this?", he demanded. "Just what the hell is this?" Shirley said: "It's Halloween . . ." Angrily, he responded: "I know what day it is, stupid, I said what is this?" still waving the bags in front of Shirley's face. She said: "Bud, they are the boys tricks and treat bags, what is the matter with you?" He came closer and closer, threateningly waving the bags closer and closer to her face." When he got close enough he hit her first with one then the other, candy was flying in all directions. She sobbed: "Don't please don't, Bud please . . ." then he threw both bags into the air and came toward her with both fists flying. "You had my kid's begging! Outside begging, from our neighbors! Damn you!" Shirley felt the explosions of pain in her head, saw colors before eyes, then nothing. When she awoke it was to find herself still on the couch. It was dark, she tried to move, but felt pain all over. She shivered, suddenly cold, as she gingerly reached down and felt her body, she was shocked to discover she was nude! She hurt all over, head, shoulders, her side, still she struggled to sit up. It was difficult, but at last she was able to sit up and let the dizziness begin to subside. Holding onto the arm of the couch she pulled herself erect. Slowly she made her way to the bathroom, closed the door and turned on the light. The shock of what she saw in the mirror was almost too much for her to face! She became sick and began to wretch. Sitting on the floor to keep from falling, she was finally able to rise and bathe herself. Avoiding eye contact with the wide eyed fright in the mirror she slowly made it to the children's room and looked inside. Looking inside from crib to crib, she was able to see by their nightlight that all four were deep in slumber land. "Thank you, God", she prayed silently. Another few steps took her to their bedroom where she could make out the outline of Bud lying across the bed. The snoring noises assured her he was asleep-or passed out. Taking an extra blanket she wrapped herself in it and fell into a dazed sleep on the couch. When she awoke, it was to the sun pouring through the window. She lay there, squinting, trying to remember what had happened. Painfully she struggled up to a sitting position. There on the floor at her feet, were the clothes she had worn the day before. Some were ripped beyond repair where Bud had obviously torn them from her unconscious body and tossed them. There, too, among the pieces of clothing were brightly wrapped candies sprinkled all around the floor. The boys trick or treat candies, she remembered. Their treasure of the day before which had brought them such happiness. It was too much, she began to disintegrate into tears. She realized that Bud had in every sense of the word raped her, but who would listen to such a statement from a wife about her own husband? She knew she was close to being at the end of her mental rope and would have to make a stand or risk even worse pain than she now had. If he were to kill her who would raise her darlings? Oh, God! Surely not Bud, with his mother stoutly standing beside him, declaring she would help him The world didn't need more little 'Bud's' that was for sure. Determined her son's would grow up as loving individuals, they would be shown love and how to live without brutal force being their most important weapons, she gathered all the inner strength she could. Slowly she crawled on her hands and knees, picking up the things strewn across the floor. Trying to divide the candies as best she could before they wakened to see what would surely shock them, she worked steadily. Bud had left the house sometime that morning, and although he never wakened her in the past, how could he leave her lying in the nude, knowing the children could have walked into find such a scene?! Ignoring her pain, she felt that he might have at least given that scenario some thought! Throughout the day she soothed the children's fears as to why mommy looked so 'funny' by telling them she had fallen down. That day she walked to the grocery with the children piled into the large buggy and used the public telephone. Once again she called the police station to see what she could do. Asking to speak to an officer, she waited, holding her breath. Soon an efficient sounding voice was speaking in her ear. She explained what had happened, including the rape, but was fearful of giving her name. When asked if this had occurred in the past she reluctantly admitted it had, and what had happened. Once he knew she had dropped the complaint the last time, he seemed to feel without a doubt, it would be the same scenario, and therefore felt he would be wasting his time as well as the courts. Tearfully she hung up, standing with her face pressed into the booth, she was shattered. The officer had even explained to her that every husband has his 'rights' and to refer to normal relations between a husband and wife as rape was ridiculous! Taking several quick breaths to try and get control of herself she went back to the children. Together the boys asked if they were going home now. "Yes", she answered, "we're going home now", while mentally she thought to herself 'home?' Home is supposed to be a haven, a place of loving, caring and safety. She had always dreaded going 'home' as a youngster, to uncaring parents, now she was a parent herself and dreaded every bit as much returning home! Once the children were taking their naps she sat down at the kitchen table, struggling mentally to rearrange her life. There had to be a better way to live than this existence. But how to go about changing things, she had no clue. They had never developed any close friendships due to the constant moving, but she'd always been content just having her children around her. You didn't many any close ties in housing projects, there was no one for her to turn to, if even for advice. All during the day she prepared and rehearsed the speech she would make to Bud when he came home that night. She was prepared with threats as well as promises, what she was not prepared for was the Bud that come in the door that night. Certainly he was not the man who had beaten and subdued and used her the night before. No, he was the young Bud she used to know. The one with the winning Irish ways. He arrived early . . . laden with packages. There was a complete dinner from a Chinese restaurant take-out! Course after course, delectable odors poured into the air! There were special treats for the children, and even a box of chocolate candy for her. She could not believe her eyes! The children were pleased—she was confused! He took Shirley into his arms, in the most gentle way, and he stroked her with words that were unbelievable. He begged her forgiveness for the night before. He said he had stopped at his mother's and she had coaxed him to stay for dinner. The whole time she told him how wonderful he was and how sad it was to be so taken advantage of, by a wife who didn't appreciate him. Finally, upset by her ravings he left and went to the tavern where he drank himself into the animal she had seen. He insisted that wasn't the real him, he wasn't a cruel person, it was the liquor added to the ravings of his mother. Looking down to the floor where the children were happily playing with their things, she wanted so much to believe him. The thought of having this loving atmosphere was the answer to all her dreams. It was so easy to accept him and his words. Too easy. Never did it dawn on her at the time that she was a threat to him! Never did she take the time to realize that he probably feared her calling the police again. Spending even one night in jail had been a chilling experience for him, he didn't know that the police had turned their backs on her pleas for help. How could he know whether or not she might get some frightening results from 'crying rape' by him? It was sometime before she put those thoughts together and then she marveled at how gullible she had been. Still, that night she did the inevitable, she forgave him. She accepted his apologies. She trusted him, that things would get better. So once again, it was time for play-acting. She never let on to anyone that there were any problems in their life. The walls in the projects were paper thin, everyone knew of everyone's quarrels, some violent, some not. Yet none of them reached out to the other, it was as though by ignoring their problems they could also ignore their own! As time passed, so did her soreness and the bruises faded as well. Soon they were notified that they were chosen to move once again. This time it would be to a location where Quonset buildings were. On going to see it for the first time they were taken aback. It seemed like a quaint little village on its own! There was a grocery store, and a school right there. On locating the address given them, they were dumbfounded to discover the past residents had built a huge porch/deck which would soon become the play spot for all the neighborhood youngsters. There was a white picket fence surrounding a well kept yard, which even included flowers. Their Quonset was divided in two, with a family on either end. Across the sidewalk was another set-up, and behind them still another, which formed a cul de sac of sorts, consisting of six families. Soon it seemed like a real neighborhood, with adults calling to each other across the sidewalk's and all the children playing together. Her youngest daughter was amazing to Shirley, she had a sweet oval face, lovely dark hair like Bud's, and such a 'good' baby everyone marveled. Her big sister would soon be 2 years old and was well on the way to becoming spoiled. The fact that after two sons he'd sired a daughter, somehow instilled something in Bud which made him think he was the only one of his kind. When he returned from work he'd walk right past the boys, over to Joyce, whereupon he would pick her up, cover her with kisses and call her Daddy's little girl. The two boys were old enough to feel rejected by his treatment and often struggled not to cry. Whenever Shirley would attempt to speak to him about how unfair this was, he'd shrug it off, because 'boy's don't need affection—girls do.' 'Boys need to be tough so they can grow up to be real men' She knew even then that the way he had been reared as a child and into his teens, was beginning to reflect in his attitude toward his own children. Still things worked out so much better after the move, even though they were an odd sight for her on her arrival, she quickly became adjusted once again. Although the buildings were made of metal, and could retain the heat, they quickly figured out an answer to that problem. The smaller families lived in oval shaped buildings that theirs had a slanted roof, resembling a small house, and by spraying the roof with their hose, they were able to control much of the heat. There were no electric fans, still it remained quite comfortable inside. There were two very large bedrooms in the back, one for the children, the other for them. They purchased maple bunk beds, where the boys slept, and Joyce slept in a bed alongside the bunks, while baby Judy slept in her crib, next to Shirley. There was a storage shed in back where lawnmowers, etc. could be stored safely away from children's hands. Johnny would be attending school in the fall, although it was only kindergarten it was something he looked forward to and Shirley began to make the arrangements. Those years were a time of experience and learning for her. Having other women to talk to during the day, while the children played was a real joy. Making women friends was completely new to her. Things in general, were much different, all the men seemed ready and willing to reach out and help one another as well. Often several would be gathered around one's car as they worked on keeping the old vehicles running. All were veterans of course, and all were struggling to make a go of their marriages and their lives. Bud still continued to drink, but not to a large extent, mostly he and the others would 'pitch in' and get beer they all shared. Everyone seemed to have so much in common. Shirley learned to drive that year, which was a passport to freedom of sorts! She could drive to the larger grocery on Saturday while Bud watched over the children, often more than one of the wives would shop together, it was a good time in their lives. Johnny only attended a half-day of kindergarten, and then it was simply a way for 5 year olds to interact with each other. There were no real learning lessons, other than tying their shoes, and learning their abc's but still, Johnny loved it. Then after only a matter of weeks he came home with a case of the chicken pox! Well, of course, it was only a matter of time before the other children had them too, although the doctor had assured Shirley the baby had a natural immunity, she too was soon covered! It seemed to Shirley that all she did was cover little bodies with lotion to relieve the itching. During this time, Shirley's mother telephoned her and asked if she might come and visit! Surprised, as it had been sometime since they'd spoken Shirley told her of the children's plight, still Rose said she would come out the following week. Meantime, Johnny had cleared up and Shirley asked the doctor if he might return to school once again, and was assured he could. He also reminded Shirley to check his chest before sending him, which she did. Horrors of horrors that Monday morning she discovered to her dismay, that he now has the beginning of the measles! School was not such a great thing after all, she thought. The following weeks all four children suffered through the measles as well. There were temperatures, baths, crying and not much sleep other than that snatched now and again, she was exhausted. When Rose arrived it was a relief for Shirley to wail of her trouble, when she came up with the most helpful piece of logic in response. With the slightest ting of sympathy she looked right at Shirley and told her: "Remember, each day they get older." Shirley asked what that meant, and was told, before she knew it they would be grown up and no bother anymore! Shirley felt terrible thinking that her children could ever be considered a bother, even though it was some consolation she admitted, in thinking that they were, indeed, getting older each day! The first Christmas they lived in the Camp was a happy one, and once the Holidays were past and Bud returned to work, Shirley decided to take the tree down. Putting the baby in her crib, and setting the other three in their room, now filled with new toys, she began the project. Finally all the lights and ornaments removed she attempted to pull the tree through the doorway, when this loud shriek blasted her ears. Dropping the tree trunk, she ran into the hallway to see little Joyce coming toward her with blood running down her face! Quickly taking her into the bathroom, gently cleaning the wound she assessed it mighty need stitches! It was a deep gash across her forehead, holding her daughter to her breast she called the boys in to find out what had happened. It seemed that as they were playing she had decided to 'clean up' and was taking one toy at a time putting it back in the toy box. When she paid no attention to their complaints, Johnny took the Bugs Bunny wooden pull toy away from her and swung it, hitting her in the head. Shocked, Shirley told them to stay put, as she ran across the sidewalk to one of her neighbors to seek their help. The woman agreed to come sit with the children while her husband drove Shirley to the nearby clinic. Upon arrival at the clinic the doctor quickly looked at the wound and said it would not need stitches, then he asked Joyce her name. When she didn't answer, Shirley said her name was Joyce.

Then the doctor asked the child how old she was, and Joyce held up her two fingers. Again, Shirley interrupted by saying she will be three in August. Looking irritated, the doctor said: "Please, mother, I am talking to the child!" Respectfully, Shirley informed him that Joyce didn't speak yet. Aghast he said: "She's dumb?!" No, Shirley quickly explained that she simply had never spoken words, only sounds, but the doctor had assured her it was simply due to the fact that she was lazy. She had older brothers, plus parents who catered to her, and so she had remained silent because she had no real need to speak! Once he finished with Joyce, and had given her a lollipop, he turned to Shirley and said he'd like to speak to her, his nurse would look after Joyce. Shrugging her shoulders in resignation, assuming he wanted to inform her how much she owed him, she followed him into his office. He surprised her by asking who her doctor was and would she allow for him to call and verify the fact that he had told her that her daughter was 'lazy'. Nodding her head, Shirley agreed he might do that, and gave him her doctors name and telephone number. He promptly made the call, and Shirley watched the emotions flow across his face as he spoke and listened. He was obviously very unhappy, but why? she thought to herself. He quickly set her straight as to why—he said for a doctor to tag a child with the tag of lazy was unbelievable. Your daughter should at least be attempting speech, at her age. Feeling embarrassed, Shirley stammered that she was not a poor mother, she had tried to get her to say even "mama" but to no avail. No, she hadn't worried, because their doctor had assured her Joyce would speak when she was ready. The young doctor shook his head in a sympathetic way and said he wasn't questioning her, but felt Joyce should be examined by another doctor. I have a friend who has a practice in the field of eye, ears, nose and throat for children, he explained, and I would be happy to call him and arrange for your little one to be seen by him. Shirley quickly began to explain that they didn't have much money, and would be unable to do that. He held his finger up and told her this would be as a favor from his friend, there would be no fees whatsoever. Just let me call him and explain the situation, alright? Agreeing to let him do that, she sat feeling very uncomfortable and wondering what Bud's reaction to all this would be. The doctor returned soon, and said his friend was very interested in seeing Joyce, then he gave her his friends name and office address. Back home again it was sometime before she realized the Clinic had not charged her! The next months were really hard on Shirley as she traveled not only to the specialist the doctor had recommended, but to Chicago for an EEG to be assured there was no brain damage, nor epilepsy. There were even a couple trips to a psychologist, which a neighboring friend drove her and Joyce to, for further testing. Now that all testing had pointed to the fact she was physically normal, Joyce saw the psychologist without her mother being present. Shirley worried she might be frightened, but just the opposite seemed true, she always came out smiling happily. At last after several of these sessions Shirley was brought into the inner sanctum to view the films they had recorded of Joyce. Seeing her little daughter happily playing with a huge dollhouse, with all kinds of furniture Shirley realized why she had seemed so happy after her sessions. They then explained how the different reactions to the toys she was given to play with, had brought them to a simple conclusion: she had to be taught to speak! Most babies learn to speak on their own by mimicking others, Joyce was unable to do that. So it would fall to Shirley to sit at least one hour a day with Joyce holding a mirror before her. Then Shirley was instructed as to which sounds to make, and how to form them with her mouth so Joyce might do the same. Shirley sat back in the large chair, staring in amazement at those two specialist, she felt troubled, even though very relieved at the same time. Seeing her frown she was asked if she had further questions, "Yes", she said she did. She asked why the dollhouse-play was used, what had that shown them? They looked at one another then back to Shirley and she was told to view the film yet again, and to pay close attention as to what she saw. As she sat there again seeing her daughter reaching for furniture, and dolls, and concentrating as she placed them, she suddenly sat up straight and gasped aloud! Even in her untrained eyes she noticed that she had chosen a mommy doll and two boy dolls, one girl doll and an infant in a cradle. She had re-created her own family Shirley saw. During the different sessions, each identified by dates on the lower half, she saw the same thing repeated, then she noted something else-the mommy doll seemed always to be in the kitchen or in the bedroom, always with the children around her. There is no daddy doll, she thought to herself, why would that be, she wondered. Once the lights were back on she turned to the two doctors and hesitatingly revealed what she had noticed. Grimly they nodded in agreement with her, then she was told she had not paid close enough attention, for while she was correct as to the mommy doll, there was indeed, a daddy doll. Questioningly Shirley said: "Really? I didn't notice him at first, then when I started to actually look I never saw one." The doctors then told her a frightening tale. They too, had noticed the lack of the daddy doll so before she left the other sessions Joyce was handed him and told to place him in the house as she had the others. After she'd left they found said doll with his head in the toilet! The next session, repeating the action, she had chosen to put him head first into the chimney! "But—I don't understand! Why would she do that? What does it mean?" she stuttered. She was advised that this type of behavior by such a little one could only mean she had a fear of her father! This really shocked Shirley, because of all four children Joyce was treated to the most affection by her father! Yet, somehow she must have sensed the fear in others, and so displayed it in this rather odd manner. They continued to practice speech for hours on end, it took time and patience, on everyone's part, but it did work. Son she was able to speak out her wants and needs, and true to his word, that doctor and all his friends never submitted a bill to the family. What incredible kindness, Shirley told them, as she wrote her warm letter of gratitude. Then in 1954 rumors began to run rampant around the Camp, that it too, would soon be closed. It would be the end to Government Projects soon. Shirley worried what would happen to them when this took place? Where would they go? One day, she voiced her fears to the other women who had gathered on her porch watching the children at play. One woman smiled and told her of their answer to the forthcoming dilemma. Because her husband was a veteran she had written to get information on how to obtain a veterans loan for housing. They were in the process of buying a house! Shirley couldn't believe her ears! "A house?" she squeaked, you're buying a house?!" The whole idea seemed so farfetched to her, her parents had never owned a house, there was surely no way her and Bud could own one, even his mother lived in an apartment! Later that day, she sought Jean out and asked her about this thing called a GI Bill, then wrote down all the information she could. The following Saturday morning, before he had anything to drink, Shirley sat down with Bud and told him of this fascinating idea. They talked a long time, she poured her heart out to him, trying to say the right things. She had realized that this might be the answer to many problems, not only would they be 60 miles away from his mother, but perhaps the responsibility of having to make payments in order to keep his own home might be the very thing to make him cut back on his drinking. Surprisingly, he was really interested in all she told him, and they drove to the sub-division that was to be built the next day! One by one, they walked through the model homes, gathered up all the brochures, floor plans and returned to the project. During the weeks to come they found many more of their neighbors were considering moving to Meadowdale, too. They made several trips, then sold all their insurance policies and even the old war bonds Shirley had saved from high school days. Finally they had amassed enough to feel comfortable to speak to the people in charge. They were treated with the utmost respect and were both impressed by the promises made to them. Soon they had put their deposit down and were making frequent trips south, picking out their style of house . . . choosing colors, etc. Then came the time when they were given a Lot number, and knew where their house would be actually located. Each trip meant more pictures being taken, Shirley was so thrilled at the whole prospect it was hard to control her excitement. As she told her parents of their future plans even they were amazed at such a fantastic plan. Never having owned a home they had no way of forewarning the young couple that dreams could quickly turn into nightmares. No one knew of the costs involved in owning a home. There were things like taxes they'd never paid before. Imagine their shock to learn they were beyond the limits of the city and so would have a huge gas tank in their yard to service their cooking and heating needs! Fortunately there was water and electricity, however each of those came at a cost, as well as garbage removal. Still, once they moved in, the thrill of putting a real home together cushioned the worry of those things. Bud continued driving to the city to work, as tuck pointing paid well and they needed a steady income. Shirley had drawn up a monthly budget for them to follow and felt confident they would have no huge problems. Then came winter and Bud was unemployed once again, still, Shirley felt they would make it through, if she just worked the few winter months as she had in the past. The great thing about being a waitress was that one could work as many hours as they chose and the better job they did, the better were the tips! She worked at a lovely restaurant where the kitchen was all stainless steel, and so clean. They served only chicken, by the quarter, by the half, with many side dishes and was especially appealing to women. Problem was, Shirley soon discovered, women didn't tip nearly as well as men! However, in this instance it didn't really mater, because they were each paid quite well and all the waitresses 'pooled' their tips so she had a fairly stable income she could count on. It was different than any other place she had worked in the past, and she was fairly content until one day fate intervened. It came in the body of a man named

Tommy, who as co-owner of the most renowned Restaurant in the area. He and a few friends were having a business lunch and Shirley served them. Afterward, as the others were leaving and Tommy handled the bill, he asked Shirley why she was working in such a low-income place. Startled she looked at him not knowing how to respond. Finally she explained she worked during the winter months to help support her family as her husband was in construction and off during that time. He handed her his card and asked her to call when she could and he would talk to her further. Flattered, Shirley thought it over for several days then finally made the call which resulted in her working at Floyd's Restaurant, which Tommy managed for his brother, Floyd. With his recommendation she was hired on the spot. Her wages were much lower than at the Chicken House, but her tips was fantastic! Some evenings she would come home with her pockets filled with change and dollar bills. She got in the habit of leaving all the change on the table and the boys would stack and sort them all each morning. They liked the ritual and it made Shirley proud to see how well they handled their 'job.' Problem was, once Bud returned to his job, it was difficult for Shirley to leave hers, and so she stayed, and hired a young teenager who lived two doors down to watch the children from the time Shirley left at 4 p.m. until Bud got home about an hour later. She made dinner and had it keeping warm in the nesco roaster so the sitter might feed them at 5 p.m. Things were going well, bills were caught up and their family life seemed good. The four children were all in school, Bud curtailed his drinking, and Shirley had high hopes for their future! Although this 3-bedroom house was not a castle she felt it more than lived up to the words of those who sold it to them. Less than $10,000 and only $54 a month payments made her dream a reality. However, during the winter months more gas was used for heating of course, and one couldn't get a ½ tank like they had with oil in the past. It became rather frightening as the bills piled up, and the fear of losing their home was ever-present. But that fear became the force that kept her going through the rough times. So happy to know her children were in their own home, had their own backyard, she was intent on keeping them there. It was worth the long and tiring hours on her feet. She took the shifts the other girls wouldn't work and came home with enough money to buy two weeks worth of groceries on those 'off' nights! Back then a $100 worth of food took them through two whole weeks, and that was eating well!

Then Bud began drinking heavily once again, although Shirley was blissfully unaware for a time. Because the children were fed at 5 if he called the sitter she would stay later, and because she lived so close, walk home once he arrived. Shirley had no way of knowing he often came home drunk and did some strange things, which she never heard about until after the children were adults! Things like pitching butcher knives at the wooden backdoor, but by the time she got home everyone was in bed, asleep, and the children never told!

During this time, Shirley began to feel tired, physically and spiritually as well. She became depressed, yet fought the feelings off. Being there to send the children off to school and when they came home, had always been top priority for her. Hers would never be key-kids like she'd been she thought, proudly. Avoiding Bud by working nights, and with him gone during the days, there had been no arguments. She drifted through life a day at a time, not knowing what was missing, but sensing something sure was. Aside from her children she had no one to speak with, other than customers, and she felt a lack of companionship. Still, she convinced herself to be non-complaining, because after all, wasn't she living the life she'd craved?! She had a home—children—what more could there be? Perhaps as the children grow older, she thought, our lives will be more satisfying. Her mother, was seldom heard from, as she had one male "friend" after the other, she was enjoying her life, and not too thrilled at being a Gram. Still, there were occasions she would be driven out by one of her friends and would always have a bag of goodies for each of the youngsters. They called her their 'shopping bag grandma' because she always came laden with things she'd found at the 'dime store.' Strange thing was, they loved all the gifts she gave them, and loved her too. Strange because Gladys, their other grandma was always seeking to buy their love, by bringing expensive gifts, yet they were a tad reluctant to accept her bags. Children are gifted with a sense that adults would be lucky to have!

Then, one afternoon as she was preparing to leave for work she was surprised to see Bud drive up early. She was happy about it because rather than spend the $2.00 for the cab to take her to work, she'd be able to drive. Going toward the backdoor to greet him, she realized immediately that he had been drinking and in fact, was quite drunk. He staggered in as she backed into the front room.

He asked where did she think she was going? Of course, without thinking, she answered: "You know what I'm going, I'm on my way to work." He began to cuss and tell her she was NOT going anywhere. In fact, he went on ranting: "You're not going to work EVER again! It's time you stayed home and be a real wife to me." A few years before Shirley would have given her right arm to be told she'd never work again . . . but not now! Not in this way! Common sense told her they could not exist solely on his wages and she told him so. Big mistake! He threatened her, but somehow his physical threats didn't frighten her as they always had before. Maybe having had that span of non-confrontations had left her foolishly unsure how to react. She looked right at him and said give me the car keys, you know we can't afford for me to lose my job. "No! No keys, you can walk!" Finally, she shrugged and said okay then, I'll call the cab like I always do, and reached for the telephone on the table next to the couch. Suddenly Bud reached across her and yanked the telephone from the wall, holding it over his head. He shouted at her: "I told you—you are staying home!" As she crouched in the corner of the couch she watched him wave the phone with the cord weaving in front of her face, like a huge snake. Trying to sound reasonable, she tried again to persuade him to let her go to work. Then his arm descended and there was an explosion of pain throughout her face and head! Waves of pain snaked through her entire body, she started to shake. She felt nauseous, dizzy and trying to stand, her legs were like rubber. The room revolving before her eyes all she could think of, 'was where are the kids?' Then she remembered they were at the sitter's as she had been about to leave for work. Then another jolt of pain rocked her. She'd seen his fist come toward her, but couldn't seem to coordinate her movements to duck! With every last ounce of strength she had, she ran past Bud, snatched up his car keys, and never stopping made it out the backdoor. She literally jumped into the car in the driveway. Looking up as she turned the key she saw Bud coming after her, the phone still in his hand. The engine caught, then stalled and died. Desperate now, she turned the key again and the engine roared into action. She jammed it into reverse and shot down the driveway and into the street! Punching the gear into drive she tore off. Looking in the rearview mirror the last image she had was of Bud standing there with that phone held high, shouting after her, as she tore off. Realizing her lungs were bursting, she'd held her breath for so long, she turned the corner, pulled over and took a few deep breaths. Shaking, tears coursing down her cheeks she thanked

God for letting her escape. Even then she knew she was hurt badly but didn't know where to go! Slowly she drove to the next town where she went to the home of an elderly gentleman who had befriended her some years before. When they had needed help the first winter she had sought him out as the Township Supervisor and requested food assistance. He had treated her kindly and with much concern had told her to come to him 'anytime' he could be of help. Well, she thought grimly I sure need help now, don't even have my purse, no money, where can I go, what can I do?

She pulled into his driveway and made her way to the door, still shaking. When he responded to the bell, the shocked look on his face told her she was looking as bad as she felt. Taking her arm, he guided her to a chair and asked: "What on earth?" She told him the truth, no making alibis for Bud this time. Bringing her a cool glass of water, he left to make a phone call. He told Shirley he had called the Police Department, and informed them of her condition and whereabouts. Because he was a retired judge he felt she should call someone to make arrangements for the children's care and then go to the courthouse to file charges. Knowing no one else to call, she called her mother-in-law and told her what Bud had done, and that she had run out to save her life, now she was concerned for the children's welfare. Listening, Gladys said she would go right out to the house and see to the children's care, although she was "sure that Shirley was exaggerating once again!" In so much pain, and overwhelmed by confused thoughts Shirley could not even argue she simply hung up in defeat! Then the judge gave Shirley some cash and told her he had called the city attorney who would drive her to the courthouse. Wanting to wash up and comb her hair she was told she should appear just as she was. Head down, feeling ashamed at how she must look, she did as he advised. The attorney listened to her story as they made the trip to the county courthouse. Soon she had a team of people surrounding her, taking pictures of her, facing this way and then that way. One of the individuals asked her what kind of an accident she'd been in! Numb, she didn't respond. After this she was driven to the nearby hospital where it was discovered, among her many injuries she had suffered a dislocated jaw, which explained why she was in so much pain. After a nights sleep, helped by some strong medication she was to be released, but again, where would she go?! At last she thought of one of the waitresses she had worked with and become friendly with, and called her. Madeline made it to the hospital in quick time, and soon decided Shirley would go home with her and spend the time mending in safety. During that time she spent most of the first days in bed, trying to regain her sense of being. Slowly she regained her health and strength, sipping soups through a straw. The first thing she needed to do, once she could speak again, would be to find out if her children were alright. "How frightened they must be", she thought. Still Gladys was their grandmother-and hopefully had handled the situation in a way to put them at ease. When, at last, the time came when she could speak clearly she called her mother-in-law only to be informed that Bud had 'given' the two girls to one friend and the two boys to another! Shocked, Shirley said he couldn't do that—they were his children, not pet's for heaven's sake! She was told, in a matter-of-fact way, that yes, they are his children so he can do what he decides is best, and she (Shirley) had nothing to say about it. She had DESERTED them, after all!

Stunned, Shirley called the attorney and was told pretty much the same thing! She would have to move back and "co-habit" with her husband if she were ever to get custody of her youngsters. She couldn't believe her ears. With all the things she had suffered in her life this was the worst. She sat thinking 'was this some kind of punishment God was using? Was this His way of punishing her for not reaching out to her own mother, who after all, was widowed?' NO! Her God was a forgiving God and she knew He had forgiven her, even if she had been unable to forgive herself over the years. Every argument they ever had, had always ended by Bud telling her the one thing she had dreaded most—if she didn't do things his way he would take the children from her. Now it appeared it was possible for him to follow through on that threat, and she had to do something to prevent it. But, what? Yet even as she questioned herself she knew. She knew what she would have to do. She would have to return—home—to where Bud was. Yes, she would have to swallows what little pride she had left, and trust in God to keep her safe for as long as it took to be free of Bud, his mother, and all they represented.

So, before she could talk herself out of it, she called Bud early that Saturday morning and told him she wanted to "come home." How did he feel about that, she asked softly, and held her breath waiting for his response. Quietly he said he knew she'd come back, it was just a matter of time. He told her he knew she couldn't just leave her children—he knew full well she'd be back! What time would she arrive he asked, so he might pick up the kid's to welcome her back. Shirley told him she was about an hour away and he agreed that would be fine. She drove the distance, frightened as to what kind of a situation she would be facing. She found she had to concentrate on her driving, it had been awhile since she'd been behind the wheel of a car. Sooner than she was ready, she turned the corner of their block. Then pulling up into the driveway she shuddered, remembering the last time she'd pulled out of that same drive. The mental picture of Bud with his upraised arm, with the phone cord dangling down, haunted her. Slowly she left the safety of the car and walked up the drive when suddenly the backdoor opened and there stood Bud! Smiling he held the door open for her, ushered her in as though she were a queen arriving for a visit. Unable to believe her eyes she walked in and watched his back as he went in front of her toward the kitchen table. He turned, still smiling, and told her come and sit down, he'd just made fresh coffee! Shocked, she sank into a chair and he called out: "Kid's look who's here!" Shyly the four children came around the corner and stood looking at her. Blinking the tears back, she held her arms out to them. They came running, hugging and kissing her, telling her how much they had missed her. Judy, the youngest looked up into her mother's eyes and asked the question they were all silently asking themselves: "Are you going to stay Mommy?" Shirley assured them she was going to stay. That she would never, ever leave them again. She asked if she had ever broken a promise from the heart and they all agreed she never had. Soon tears were being shed by all, out of relief, as they took turns hugging their mother. What joy!

After a few more minutes, Bud spoke up quietly, saying that now that they knew they would have their mommy for the rest of their lives, because she just promised them that, could he have sometime with her now? Obediently, they trooped into the living room and made a semi circle around the TV set. Bud poured two cupfuls of coffee then sat across from Shirley. Here it comes, she thought, here come the rules, keep your mouth shut! Just nod your head in agreement to whatever he says. Remember, in the end, no matter how long it may take, someday you'll be free of him. You and the kid's will have no rules to follow, just listen and nod. To her great surprise, though no rules were forthcoming. Matter of fact he told her how sorry he was to have injured her as he had. She was stunned to know he even knew of the dislocated jaw and the many meals taken through a straw. It seemed that Madeline had made a few phone calls of her own, and while she told bud of Shirley's injuries and pain, that she was hospitalized, she'd refused to disclose the location. He never knew how she had spent the time recuperating in Madeline's home, assuming she'd been hospitalized all that while. Gratefully, Shirley said yet another prayer of thanks for her friendship once again. But the surprises didn't stop there, he went on to say that "a judge" had called him and advised him he was legally liable for all the terrible deeds he'd committed. Soon she began to realize Bud was more frightened than she was! For while she was scared to death of losing her children—he was scared of losing his freedom! So the two began to layout the mutual ground-rules for a return to their "married life."

PART III

REALITY

UNLIKE IN THE movies, or in some romantic novel, life does not always go "and so they lived happily ever after." No, life did go on, but in a much more realistic way. Shirley knew in her heart of hearts any love she might have felt for Bud was entirely gone. Sadly, she knew she could never trust him again, and so she began living two lives. One, to any outsider, they seemed like any other married couple, struggling to make ends meet. Trying to keep the bills paid, and raising their children. But two, was the woman who began to prepare for a life as a single mother. She began to withhold some of her tip money saving toward a divorce that simply had to come. She spoke with Mr. Quaig the attorney who had seen her through her terrible times, explaining she had gone back to Bud in order to someday be free of him, yet have her children by her side. He nodded in agreement and told her that his retainer fee was $50 which would get things started, but when it came to the actual divorce, her husband would be forced to pay it! What a great relief that was to Shirley. So monthly she would stop by the office and give $5 toward this end. Bud continued to work in Chicago as a tuck pointer, and also continued to stop by his mother's on a regular basis, as she was not welcomed by Shirley. One day Shirley was surprised to get a call from her asking to speak to Bud. Of course, he wasn't home yet and Gladys asked if she knew if her TV was fixed yet. Shirley had no knowledge of her TV and said she'd have Bud call her.

Then she called the nearby TV repairman who was a friend of Bud's and asked him if he had her mother-in-laws TV. She was told he did have it, but sold it because Bud had told him to! When Bud came home Shirley asked him about it, and was told to mind her own business. Well, your mother called, asking, so I called Ben and he told me he'd sold it, as you told him to! He said he had already given you the money. Well, this really set Bud off! He wanted to know why she hadn't just stayed out of his business . . . and he better teach her to do just that. Coming toward her with his fist ready to strike, Shirley ran into the bedroom and slammed the door. Before she knew what was happening he was lying across her body on the foot of the bed. She tried to get out from under him but her struggles just turned him into a wild man. A couple of open-handed slaps and she lay back trying to get her breath, and he threatened to take care of her once and for all. Then he ripped off her skirt, and still atop her began to have his way, his pants around his ankles, there they were, when the kid's came running down the hall! Shirley screamed for them to go to their rooms—go! They did! They went! Which of the children was it? What had they heard? What had they seen? As she lay there enduring the physical punishment her mind screamed: "What had they seen!" After he finished, Bud lay there spent and passed out! When she was sure he was unconscious, Shirley squeezed out from under him, closed the door and went to find the children, who were all in their beds. Puzzled, she wondered if she had imagined they had been in the doorway, then locking up, she took a warm bath and slept on the couch. When she awoke in the morning he had left for work without waking her. Life went on as before, with Shirley trying to avoid Bud as much as possible, but within a short time she knew—She knew without a doubt! She was pregnant! How could she be? She had her 2 boys and 2 girls, as she'd dreamed of. Judy was getting older she was 4 already, soon be old enough for kindergarten, all four would be in school. She couldn't be pregnant now. Not now! But she was! Finally she told Bud they would be having a baby the following March, waited for his explosion, but instead he was pleased as punch! Raving about how he was a 'real' man he took off to the tavern to brag to his drinking pal's while Shirley wept into her pillow! The pregnancy was a long 9 months for Shirley. She went to her Attorney and ashamedly admitted she was expecting her 5th child, soothingly he told her not to worry, as "the spoon will was still in the soup" . . . Huh? What did that mean? It meant, he said, that when the child was born she could still go on with her planned divorce. She thanked him and left, dejectedly. How could she possible think divorce, here she was pregnant. How long could she work? So many questions! No answers. During that pregnancy Shirley lost 18 pounds! No weight gain. She worked as long as she was able, and all her co-workers pitched in and 'showered' her with gifts for the baby to be. They gave her a new crib and mattress and filled it with sheets and blankets and the men, bartenders, bus boys, pitched in and gave her 6 months worth of diaper service! The neighborhood women even gave her a show, gifting her with much new clothing all in green and yellow, because, of course no one could foretell the sex of the expected baby. Along came the month of March and along came a beautiful baby boy! He had light blonde hair, lovely blue eyes and Shirley was constantly told he was "too pretty" to be a boy! It was all amazing to Shirley, and although it had been such a shock at the beginning she welcomed this new little life with open arms and heart. Judy began school that fall and so Shirley had the baby all to herself for each day, and she loved it! Reasoning returned and she began to realize that Mr. Quaig was right she still could be a single mom, it just might take a little longer, but by golly she would do it! Someday! Reality was, after all, reality!

Because reality had also shown Bud that Shirley would need to work to be able to keep the house, she returned to work. But because she had been gone for such a long period while recuperating, she had lost her status at the restaurant. One day Tommy called her in to the office and told her he needed a favor of her, unsure of what he needed, she just nodded. Feeling grateful he had taken her back at all, she was willing to pay him back, however it was a huge favor he sought!

His cousin owned a small restaurant in the next town, the town where her judge friend lived, and where her attorney had his office. The problem was, they had no 'head waitress' only some gal's who were used to 'slinging has' as he stated. Tommy had told his cousin that he knew of a woman who could train any waitress into becoming a good worker. It was Shirley he had in mind! She was hurt to think she would be so little thought of, as to be turned out to work in a Pizza/Bowling Alley place! Actually she felt a bit insulted as she mulled it over. Seeming to understand what she was thinking, Tommy told her to have a seat as he explained what he had in mind. This would only be a temporary thing, and he would see that she was paid enough to cover her loss of the larger tips she was now receiving, working at

Floyds. He went on to praise her work ethics and to flatter her to the point that she finally gave in, and agreed to make the change. So, that began another phase of her life for Shirley. That fall was a busy time for her as she slowly and patiently as possible, explained how a "good" waitress worked. There was a second floor, just as in Floyd's and it was converted into a Banquet Room where large parties could be served. For although it was a Pizza place, they also served steak, chops and chicken dinners. The business began to really take off, and everyone was pleased. The good part for Shirley was that her wages having been raised she had a steady income she could rely on—plus her tips which were beginning to show a marked difference than when she had first arrived. Soon, Mr. Quaid had his full retainer fee, and he announced to her that he would begin to process her divorce. She was thrilled. However, the bad part was he didn't inform her that a Sheriff's Deputy would be serving the papers to Bud! Although over time Shirley had told Bud she just couldn't continue living as they had been. She was tired of his tantrums which sometimes turned into insanity. She was tired of herself always cowering whenever anyone raised a hand to reach for something. He said he knew she was right but still didn't quite believe she would actually follow through! Then one night, with Shirley and the older boys at the kitchen table where they were doing their homework, the girls in their room, and the baby in bed, there came a loud knock on the door. Bud, sitting in the living room watching TV, got up to answer it . . . and there, in the doorway, a lit flashlight in his hand stood a Deputy! He asked Bud his name, and then served him with the divorce papers. Shirley froze in place! Quickly she sent the boy's to their room, only to look up into Bud's livid face as he stood there with the papers crumpling in his hand! She tried to speak, what she was going to say she didn't know, but she never got the chance anyway. He swung at her and papers went flying, as he came in contact with her head. She begged him to stop it, but he shoved her across the floor and onto the couch where she half lay, half sprawled, her hands up over her face. As he went toward her, two tornadoes came flying across the room! There were John and Jim, attacking him with their fists flying as they tearfully cried: "Leave Mommy alone." A shocked Bud fell to his knees and started to hit them, when Shirley became a mother-tiger! Never had she tired to fight back, but these were her children and she became a wild woman! She screamed at him to get out! Get out now or I'll call the police and you'll be in jail for more than an overnight visit!" He stood there, shocked, looking from her to the two boys who with tears in their eyes were still standing ready to protect their mother. At last, without a word, he turned and left. Shirley sat down in relief, and hugging her son's told them everything would be all right. Then she went and locked the doors, and told them to go to bed, following her own advice, she did the same. She lay there for a long time before sleep finally claimed her.

The next morning, to her immense relief, Bud never appeared nor did he call. The children went to school and she cleaned up the house. Then she called Mr. Quaig to tell him what had happened. He was very apologetic, and told her to call him at once if Bud should appear, and he would be alerting the local police to be aware of a potential problem. One night the following week she was at work when she was alerted by one of her co-workers that there was a phone call for her, and it sounded like her husband! Did she want him to listen in on the extension? Looking as frightened as she felt she urged him to do just that. Then both of them were shocked to hear Bud's drunken voice screaming at her, wanting to know where she had taken HIS children? Why weren't they in the house? He would find them, and drag them one by one, down the middle of the street by their hair! She would regret this, he promised. She would be sorry, then shaking she hung up the phone! Quickly she called Mr. Quaig and left for her neighbor's where she had left the children for their safety . . . 'just in case' . . . finding them safe and unaware. Thankful she had the forethought she then headed for her home where the police were to meet her. When she arrived she saw there were two squad's on either side, without lights, but with officers in both. As soon as she pulled up, they jumped from their squads and advised her they would accompany her into the house, per Mr. Quaig's instructions. Seems he had filed a 'quit claim deed' which did not allow for Bud to be on the property. Shirley reached for the door when her key in hand, only to find the door was ajar. Pushing her gently aside, the officers preceded her, motioning her to remain silent. As they went down the hallway they found Bud passed out on the bedroom floor, with a cigarette burn next to his head.

One on each side, the officers roused him, not too gently, and ordered him on his feet. Then as he stood, dazed they handcuffed him. He looked down at a shaken Shirley, and holding up his cuffed hands said: "Look, what you have done to me!" The one officer told him he had done this to himself, and they were taking him to the police station. Now. Telling Shirley to follow them, they drove off. Arriving at the station, a trembling Shirley walked inside to find no Bud in sight, but Mr. Quaig waiting for her with a sad smile on his face. He had been filled in on the situation and told her she could return home, and bring her children there as well. They would be safe for Bud would be incarcerated for a time. That would be the last time Shirley would see Bud until they were at the Courthouse, for the divorce. When he arrived he had his mother on one side, and a young woman on the other, whom Shirley could not identify. The judge granted the divorce and full custody of the children and the house to Shirley. Relieved and gratified, Shirley went up to Mr. Quaig to thank him, then as she turned the young woman who had been with Bud came up to her. With a face contorted with anger she said to Shirley that what she had just done to 'poor Bud' was a terrible thing. Taking his children from him. How could she?! She couldn't believe the accusations Shirley had made against a wonderful man who she had known for sometime and hoped to marry. Stunned, Shirley looked at her and wished her well, and Good Luck as she would surely need it! Then turning on her heel she caught up with Mr. Quaig and her ride home. That was a long ride for Shirley as she tried to accept the fact she really was divorced. Free from Bud and his mother. Now she would have to work extra hours to keep the house the judge had ruled to be hers. She knew she must be able to keep that house, because her children deserved a home. A home filled with love and laughter, not the terrible times they had endured in their young lives.

One day the chef where she worked was cleaning up the kitchen while his wife waited to drive him home. Shirley was cleaning up her station as well, and offered the woman a cup of coffee. They began to talk about the lack of money both of them were suffering through, and Delores approached Shirley with a way to earn extra cash. Delores enjoyed making appetizers and wondered if Shirley would like to join her in creating varied types of crustless sandwiches, etc. Her idea being she would make contact with people who were in need of such creations, for weddings, showers, etc. If Shirley would join her and do the actual making and freezing these items she, Delores, would take on the chore of delivering them. They would invest equally in the supplies, bread, relishes, etc. and would in turn, split the profits. To Shirley it sounded like an answer to prayer, and she promptly agreed. The next day, she and Delores spent hours going over the arrangements for this small business they were anxious to begin. Shirley got into the habit of coming home from her nightshift, and sitting at the kitchen table for an hour or tow, creating varied types of canapés, hors d'oeuvres, fancy sandwiches. One night she would create several spreads the next night the sandwiches themselves. Her freezer was filling up! Delores held up her end of the bargain, seeking people in need of such a service and delivered them when due. It was workable and a part of the solution as to how Shirley could manage to keep the house payments up, as well as utilities. Plus she was there when the children left for school and there when they returned which continued to be her goal. She had sat on her bed with a son on each side, and explained what it would mean, being divorced from their father. She'd warned them it would be difficult at times, financially especially, and they would have to be there to help her as they could with the three younger ones. Soberly they nodded their heads and agreed that this would be best for everyone. True to their word, the boys pitched in, and after bringing John into the lawyers office for 'an interview' she was told he was responsible enough to look after his siblings while she was at work. That meant no longer paying a babysitter! Money saved!

Days passed, then weeks, then months. Life was actually easier on all of them, the fear was gone and they were able to relax. Once school started Shirley was able to get a nap during the day and continue to work at night. She ran an ad in the newspaper and would type out resumes and other papers for the students of the local community college. Small amounts of cash were earned this way to add to that from the canapés business. Soon the bills were caught up and although there wasn't a lot of money 'leftover' for extras they managed to have fun times. Often, as a special treat Shirley would drive them to a place nearby that was actually a deserted old home, but resembled a castle. The boys would break off large stemmed weeds which quickly became their swords as they 'dueled' for their sisters had become princesses to be rescued! Once, after a particularly fun time, young Jimmy hugged her and told her that some day HE would have a real castle and then she could live there with him! Who could have guessed that a 'castle' would become reality in the distant future? But it did! Often there would be an excursion to the next town which offered special 3-decker ice cream cones. They would go to the many local parks and play areas, like the one that held an old fire engine to play on. It was a fun time. Sometime during that year of 1959 Shirley had become aware of a male customer who came in for dinner on a regular basis. For some reason she just took a dislike to him but didn't know why. The bartender, Al, who was a cousin of her boss, asked her to be a little nicer to him because he was going through a tough time. "Right!" Shirley responded sarcastically, "poor, poor guy! I serve him, that's all I have to do, I'm not his mother." Well, she was informed that he would soon be a part of their family as he had been hired to manage the adjoining bowling alley. Then she began to notice how his eyes stared hungrily at any youngsters that came in to dinner with their parents, it worried her. Maybe he's some kind of freak, she thought, and finally shared those thoughts with Al. That's when she learned his wife had deserted him, walked out and taken his two children out of state, and he was unable to locate her or them. Shirley listened, and thought maybe, just maybe she might have misjudged him, still . . .

Shirley hadn't realized how much anger she carried, how she'd developed this deep mistrust and near hatred toward men. Then one day Al took it upon himself to introduce her to that customer, whose name was Joe. Trying to be civil, she just nodded, then walked away to see to another customer. Returning to her station she found Joe sitting there, waiting for her. Then he asked her if he had somehow angered her, by saying or doing something? He declared he certainly hadn't meant to be rude and hoped he would be forgiven. Shocked, Shirley looked into his big, brown eyes which were looking straight into her own, and knew she had been caught! She had been deliberate in her rudeness, in attempting to not be friendly, and here he was apologizing to her! Feeling her face redden, she mumbled something about not knowing what he was talking about. No, he hadn't said or done anything, she just was working not looking to make friends. Even to herself, she knew she was beyond rude now, but stood her ground until he walked away. That night, at closing, Joe came over to the restaurant from the bowling alley and invited her to join him and several others who were going across the street to the little 24-hour café for coffee. Surprised, Shirley shook her head in refusal, yet as Al and two of the other waitresses came toward her smiling she knew she would join them after all. There were other times when the group would move across the street, trading stories about different customers and winding down from a busy night. One of those nights while walking her to her care Joe told her of losing his children and how blessed she was to be able to go home to hers. Yes, she agreed, she was blessed, but what had he done to drive his family away?! "You say your wife deserted you, took your children, but believe me, I know there are always two sides to every story. No woman leaves a good husband, you must have driven her away." Even as the words left her mouth she regretted sounding so harsh, but before she could say anything further, Joe stopped, right there in the middle of the street and looking stricken, responded in a cracking voice: "You are so wrong Shirley! So wrong! I don't know much about you, other than Al says you are divorced and have several children but I sure know the angry part of you! Someone must have hurt you pretty bad for you to be as you are and I truly feel sorry for you! God help you!" and with those last words flung at her, he turned and went to his own vehicle. An open-mouthed Shirley was left standing in the street as he drove off. The next day was her day off and Shirley had plenty of time to think over what had transpired the night before. She began to question herself as to why she even cared. What did it matter to her, if this guy was upset at her accusations? Who cared? Slowly, she began to realize SHE cared. She cared that she could have been so cruel and hurtful, and knew that somehow she would have to make an apology that Joe would understand and accept. As she finished the last batch of canapés and stored them in the freezer she smiled to herself. What was happening to her? She had kept herself like this freezer—cold and unapproachable—and now? Once again she asked herself that question: "and now?' What now?!

She hadn't had to worry how to approach Joe the next night, because before she had even begun work, he came up to her. He stood in front of her, held up a piece of paper, folded it and put it in her apron pocket. With a soft smile, he simply said: "Read this when you get home and have time. I need for you to read it, Okay?" When she nodded her head yes, he turned on his heel and left. She never saw him again that evening, he must have left through the bowling alley exit she thought to herself. Too bad, she never got to apologize as she'd intended to, but perhaps tomorrow?!

A tired Shirley got home that evening, and after checking on the sleeping youngsters, returned to the kitchen to empty her uniform and apron pockets of all her tip money. As she withdrew a handful of bills, mixed in was a slip of folded paper. "Joe!" she thought. Being so busy she had forgotten all about the paper he had asked her to read. Slowly she Sunk onto the kitchen chair and opened the note. She had to re-read it because at first she had assumed it was a message for her. But no, Joe had entrusted her with something even more important! Written in a feminine handwriting it was obviously the last words he had gotten from his wife, before she had left for parts unknown. In it, she stated that while he Had "always been a good husband and a good father" she knew he would never be able to afford to give her all the things she wanted and felt she deserved. "Incredible!", thought Shirley, who had never known the life this woman had led. With a husband who went to work, came right home, turned over his paycheck so she could pay the bills. No drinking. No beatings. Instead, it seemed she had taken not only his children, but his pride as well! She had kept the last several paychecks and used that money to fly to another state. He soon lost his home due to an unpaid mortgage that he wasn't even aware of, as she had kept the warning letters from him. What a cruel person, to even tell him he had performed as a good husband and father! There seemed no excuse for such actions. Tears welled in her eyes as Shirley recalled the hurtful things she herself had said to him. How could she ever explain? Would he forgive her? He had an 8-year-old son and a daughter nearly three, and lost them both. She couldn't help but remember how she had felt when there was a chance she might lose her own darling children. And he had lost his, with no way to fight back. "Oh, Joe, I'm so sorry", she cried softly with her head on the table.

Shirley knew when she returned this letter to Joe she had many questions, but did she dare to ask them? Would she accept his answers? She didn't know, but realized she would need to seek the answers before she opened her heart to this man with whom she felt not only sympathy but something much deeper, and frightening.

The next night, Joe finished up before Shirley had her station done so he invited her to join him across the street. As she entered the café the strong smell of coffee tweaked her nose and she broke into a smile. Joe turned on his stood at the counter, and returning her smile asked what was so funny? "Well", Shirley replied, here I have been on my feet for 8 hours serving coffee across the street and now I find myself walking over here to have a cup!" They both laughed together at the irony of it.

She handed him the letter and somberly said she had read it through. Taking it from her, he nodded. Over time, every question she put to him, Joe answered sincerely. He was an honest and forthright person she soon found out. Several of the men who worked with him had nothing but good things to say about him. She began to feel frightened by the surge of feelings running through her, yet she stayed.

They stayed and they talked, about many things and the more they talked the more she accepted the pull this man had on her. The little theatre next door to the café was showing "South Pacific" and Shirley mentioned she was intending on seeing it, because it had always been her dream to someday go to Hawaii. Was that a foolish dream, she asked him? To want to go to some Island in the Pacific? He hastily reassured her it was not and spoke of how he had served there during WWII while in the Navy, and hesitantly added maybe someday he might be the lucky one to take her there. "To Hawaii? or to the movie?" she asked. Laughing along with her he suggested they might go to the movie first! Shocked at her own audacity, Shirley lowered her eyes and sipped her coffee. Then Joe asked her if she would join him on their next night off. She agreed. Later, on the way home she began to second-guess herself. Maybe she agreed to readily. Maybe—Even though she'd weighed the possibility of not going, they actually did go to see South Pacific. The music transcended them both into their own private thoughts and it was an abrupt goodnight they said when it was over. Shirley had refused to have him come to the house to pick her up and had met him at the theatre, so as she drove home she found herself humming the melodies she'd just heard. The next day she went to the Shopping Center where she purchased the sound album from the movie and played it until it was time to go to work. Later, she was to learn Joe had done the same thing!

The next night they worked they never saw one another, both being busy with their customers. The following day she was surprised by a telephone call from Joe. With the little one still at home, taking a nap, she sat and talked with him for some time. She had learned he lived with his parents some distance away, near O'Hare airport and he learned of her fears of her ex-husband someday returning to harm her children. It became a habit for him to call each day, and they grew to know one another in this manner. Their time at work was just that, work! So they had little time for more than a passing word or two. Slowly a relationship was formed through these phone calls.

Then one night the unthinkable happened, Bud showed up at the house. Of course the locks had been changed but as he stood outside yelling for the kid's to "Open up!" John called his mother at work to ask what to do. Of course she told him not to open the door and that she would be there shortly. With shaking hands, she then called the police. When she arrived home there was no one there but the children. A relieved Shirley asked them what had happened and they told her a policeman had come and told their dad to leave. "And he did!" the boys chimed. "He left!" Relieved though she was, Shirley worried if this was going to happen again and again?! What could she do? What should she do? Even as those thoughts raced through her brain, she soothed over the episode to the children and told them there was nothing to worry about. But, was there?! The next day when Joe made his daily call to her he brought up the fact that he was aware of what had happened the night before. (The worker who had answered John's phone call, had told him.) Biting her cheeks to keep from breaking down she assured Joe that all had been taken care of, and she felt the kid's were safe. His next words shocked her! He suggested he come by and sit with the youngsters until she got home each night. (The bowling alley usually shut down earlier than the restaurant.) She told him she couldn't possibly ask him to do that, he had such a long drive to his parents. Yet, he insisted, she hadn't asked—he had volunteered. So that began a period of time where Joe spent more time with Shirley's children than he had with her. The children all took to him, loved him for different reasons. The younger ones needed a father-figure, and the older two were relieved to having to be 'in charge', especially when it came to changing their little brother's diapers!

After the divorce Shirley had actively sought out a church. When her and Bud had their arguments, then the beatings that ensued, she had gone to the priest and begged him to be of help to her and her family. However, he told her she had offended God by marrying a non-Catholic in the first place, so there was nothing he could do for her. After that, she went from church to church, and one day attended a Service in a Lutheran church. She had begun bringing the children and had them enrolled in Sunday school. She took the 6-week classes and became a member, and once again felt close to her God.

One evening, as the warmer days of summer came, Joe had mentioned to the children that he would like to take them to a nearby lake to swim and picnic someday. Would they like that? Would they?! Shirley barely got out of bed the next morning and they were telling her what Joe had said. When he called that day she chided him about asking her children "on a date" and forgetting to run it past her! He chuckled and explained they had all said how they loved playing in the water and soon it would be summer vacation and one thing led to another, and . . . I'm sorry, I hope you're not too angry? "Angry?" Shirley retorted she thought it sounded great, especially if she were to come along!

Soon it was summer vacation and they made the following Sunday the day to go to Wauconda Lake. Everyone was excited at the prospect. The weather was perfect. Joe bought little Jerry a ducky-inner tube so he could sit by the shore, yet be safe in the water like his sisters and brothers. He bought other things to play with and joined them all, enjoying the water and sand himself. Shirley looked on in admiration as he so effortlessly had all five children happily splashing around then she joined in. She felt like she was living in a dream. But soon, the dream would become a nightmare!

As they pulled in the driveway of her home, Joyce was hopping from one foot to the other, having to go potty. So, handing her the backdoor key, Shirley began to get Jerry out of his car seat, when there was suddenly complete silence. Startled, Shirley looked to see what had happened—and there stood Joyce, on the doorstep, legs crossed at the ankles, in a large puddle. Jumping from the car she handed Jerry over to Joe and ran to comfort her tearful little girl who obviously had not made it to the bathroom in time! As she put her arms around the child's shoulders she realized Joyce was shaking and knew this was more than the mishap she'd originally believed. "What is it? What's wrong, honey?" Shirley demanded, shaking Joyce gently. Looking up at her mother, with tears running down her little cheeks, she said: "HE'S in there, oh momma, he's in there!" Returning Joyce to the car she asked Joe to stay with the kid's until she could find out what was going on.

Although as their eyes met, both felt they knew what was awaiting her, she begged him to stay with the children. Holding her breath she slowly entered the house. As she passed through the kitchen, there was her typewriter-table bent and broken in the space between it and her living room. The typewriter lay on the floor in front of the front door, below the huge hole it had made. As she made her way past these, she noted Jerry's highchair, an aluminum one, bent in many pieces laying up against the couch. Scattered all around the room were bits and pieces of blue and white looking like confetti. Later, she found it was Bud's copies of his divorce papers. Slowly walking past the children's rooms, she approached her bedroom, where once again she found Bud passed out on the floor in almost the same place he'd been so long ago—or was it yesterday?! Backing out, gasping for breath she got in the car and told Joe to drive her to the police station. On the way she explained it was Bud, he'd broken in, was passed out and he—trying hard to regain her sanity as visions of the broken things flashed through her mind—she sat a moment in silence. Then realizing how quiet it was, knowing the children must feel more frightened than ever, she turned to them, to reassure them as best she could. "It will be alright", she promised, as she looked from one to the other, helplessly wondering if their lives would ever be 'all right'!

As they pulled in front of the police station, Joe reached over to put his hand on her shoulder. He told her not to worry, he would take the kid's over to the park and be back for her in an hour. "Do what you "have to do", he said, exerting a reassuring pressure on her shoulder . . . "but-before you go . . ." he turned to face the children huddled together in the backseat. John and Jim sitting up straight, Joyce and Judy with a sleeping Jerry on their laps stared at him. Looking from one to the other he questioned: "How would you kid's feel if I married your mother? If I took care of all of you? What do you think?" Shirley took in a quick, stunned breath as she heard him repeat: "Well?" What do you think? John, always the big brother, asked: "Would you live with us? Would you like to be our father?" "Yes, to both questions", Joe answered.

The shocked silence of before turned into near bedlam, waking little Jerry who looked around, with questioning eyes. All four of the older children reached to pat Joe's back, telling him: "Yes, Yes" in unison. Smiling, Joe released his hold on her shoulder and quietly urged her to go. Slowly, she left the vehicle and walked toward the station doors as they drove away. "Oh God, let me not have just dreamed that, let it be true, she prayed silently. Then, squaring her shoulders, she pulled open the big doors and entered the place she hoped never to enter again.

That day would live in Shirley's memory for the rest of her life. Not because it was the last time to enter that building ever again. Not because it was the last time she would lay eyes on Bud again, although that was a huge plus. Not because it was the first of many days spent at Wauconda and other lakes, although it had shown Shirley how much Joe and the children loved one another. Not even because her children had been afraid—for themselves, for her. No, not for any of those important facts, but for the most important reason of all: Joe had proposed marriage! (Although to her children and not directly to her, Shirley loved his thoughtfulness, and knew she loved him as well.)

She'd worried how she would be treated but the officers were very kind and respectful, drove her to the house where they led a handcuffed Bud back to the squad. He looks as dazed as I feel, Shirley thought. But for far different reasons. He is rapidly going downhill, losing his life to alcohol—and me? I'm going uphill and regaining life once again as a married woman and a mother. She marveled at the thought.

On August 12, 1960, Shirley became Mrs. Joseph Kiss, there at St. Stephens' Lutheran Church, where she discovered Joe used to belong years before! After the ceremony, where at last she was able to stand before God and make her vows, she was embarrassed to hear her son ask the Pastor can we call Joe "Dad" now?! Holding her breath, waiting for his response, the tall, gentleman bent down to their level and said yes, of course they could, because in every way but through blood he would be their Dad from this day on.

"What joy!" Shirley thought: "A new name! A new life! Praise God!"

T HEY NIGHT THEY wed, they went home to bedrooms filled with five happy
children. A strange but wonderful "honeymoon."

It was difficult at first, trying to get settled into a 'normal' family, but because
they had reached the decision that both parents would agree on any issues with
the children there was never anytime when one was 'used' against the other.
Because she had taken two weeks off work to get settled in, she quickly found how
wonderful it could be to be home all day, not just send the children to school then
try and nap with Jerry, so she could go to work that night. Then one night shortly
before her vacation ended Joe asked her if she would let him know which door she
would be using when she went back to work. Confused, Shirley could only question
him: What?!" "Well," he told her if you leave by the back I might want to go out the
front because I hate to see you work outside our home! I would love things to go on,
with you staying home." That was such a unique thing to hear, Shirley burst into
tears! Feeling such gratitude she was speechless! Joe assumed she was frustrated,
because she really wanted to go back to her job, so he pulled her close and patting
her back reassuringly, told her if she really wanted to work he would of course,
understand. Tears turned into laughter as she told him the real reason for her
behavior. That same day Shirley went and spoke to her old friend/boss and told
him she wasn't coming back. He surprised her by smiling and saying he actually

wasn't surprised, and due to the fact she'd done such a great job in training the girls, setting schedules, etc. he gave her a bonus as a departing gift!

So began a new life for Shirley and her family.

Then one morning she woke up feeling extra good! Just filled with happiness, not knowing why. Soon, however she knew, the reason was she was pregnant! With Joe's baby, how wonderful! In June of '61 Julie was born, and in April of '63, Joe, Jr. was born. With an inner feeling that somehow she had given Joe the gift of two young ones 'to fill the void' of the two he had lost, pervaded her thoughts. About this time the Bowling Alley/Restaurant was sold and Joe lost his employment. Desperate, knowing seven youngsters were dependent on him, he tried every job he could. He tried selling life insurance but felt the company was too 'hard-sell' for him to cope with. He told Shirley he just couldn't push insurance onto young couples who barely had enough money for rent and food. He tried other sources, then the opportunity to work at a nearby chemical plant starting up, came. He was hired immediately due to his Navy trained experience. The salary was amazing and things really began to look up.

Soon, John was off to college, having earned a few scholarships as well as savings of his own he was soon enrolled at the University of Illinois. The following year Jim joined him through the same method.

Time passed, and Joyce and Judy both married their high school sweethearts, the family was growing, thought Shirley. Then, in May, Judy had her firstborn, a son and Shirley thought she must have reached heights in life that she never dreamed possible. Looking down at her grandson's face she could barely believe this was her grandchild. She, who had prayed just to see her children become adults, had now seen further into a future she never thought possible. Life was, indeed, good!

Then, once again, came another upheaval! Joe's place of employment was going to build an entire new plant, and they wanted Joe to be involved in its beginnings. Because Joe really loved the work, not to mention the great wages, there really was no choice but to follow Joe explained to a stunned Shirley. Well, actually there were TWO choices, he continued, they could move to McCook or Morris, IL—what was her choice? Because Shirley had become used to living in a small-town atmosphere, she felt moving closer to the City was not an option she would like, so then began the hunting for a new home in Morris. Morris, some 30 miles west of Joliet, 30 miles east of Ottawa, on I-80 and Rte. 47. After living in the same house for nineteen years, becoming a grandmother for the first time, moving was not something she savored, yet . . .

Joe's job included him working shift work, always had, and they had enjoyed what they called his 'long weekends' by going camping or taking trips with the three children still at home. Jerry was now finishing his junior year in high school, yet he chose to join his parents and two younger siblings to move to Morris too. Now they would use Joe's long weekends to house hunt! Again, turning to God, Shirley prayed they would find a suitable place to once again call 'home'.

Although the move had her filled with anxiety, remembering how she had thought she'd never live to see her children become adults. How she had left notes all over the house that in the event of her (sudden) death the children not be separated, nor given to Bud to raise. Remembering her fear for them, how could she not accept this move, when it was for Joe, who had made her and her children's lives livable?!

The actual "house hunting" turned out not to be so difficult, after all. Reason being there were so few homes available. How ironic, she thought, houses were selling like wildfire where they were leaving so the prices were scaled down, and here, in Morris only a handful of homes to choose from. Although they had searched in nearby communities they were fortunate to drive past a house "for sale by owner". This, turned out to be what they had been looking for, "Thank you, God", she murmured as they walked through the house.

They brought the three children down to see their new home, and found to their surprise the two boys had far different ideas as to their bedrooms. It was a three-bedroom ranch style home, but Jerry saw the huge room downstairs as his and his brothers! It had three walk-in closets already in place and with paint and drapes it would be ideal he insisted. When Shirley protested stating she didn't want them in the basement, his immediate response was: "It's downstairs, Mom, not a basement." So it was settled. Julie took the bedroom across from the master bedroom and the "extra" room would serve as a guest room in the future.

Because school had already begun, the first day they moved in Shirley drove Joe to work so as to take the car and enroll all three children. Jerry, as a high school senior, Julie as a 7th grader in jr. high, and Joey a 5th grader in the grade school settled in nicely. Once again, Shirley breathed a sigh of relief, they were, after all, only an hour or so away from the rest of the family. Besides, they had a lovely home, huge yard, and it became a time for her work on painting, and getting their new home cozy for the coming winter months.

October came and all the painting was done, the furniture placed, drapes hung and one morning Shirley had company. A young woman came to the door with a huge basket over her arm, announcing she was 'The Welcome Wagon Lady'. Shirley invited her in and received many small gifts and coupons for the local stores. Among other items was a newsletter telling of all the available service's which listed an organization called We Care. Questioning what this was about, Shirley was told it was something like FISH, was she familiar with it? Yes, Shirley had volunteered for FISH where she came from. That night Shirley mentioned to Joe she'd like to call their number and volunteer to be what they termed 'a Phone Volunteer' . . . what did he think? He wondered why she would want to do that, not understanding that this new town left her with no friends or family to speak to during the day. He was at work. The children all in school, she was lonely and bored. Maybe she could even help someone although she had no vehicle to drive around she would still be active in this way. Joe's only comment was he hoped she wouldn't become so involved she would be gone at night! Next day she called the number and spoke to a woman with a pleasant voice, who informed her all she would have to do is answer any calls for assistance that might come, she wouldn't have to leave her home. Once she agreed to become a Volunteer that same woman gave her several sheets of the many Volunteers who actually did perform the services needed, as well as Report Forms to be filled out and mailed to their P.O. Box. These Volunteers gave transportation to and from medical facilities, and some even offered their homes to strangers needed a place to spend the night! She was to begin her stint the following day. How exciting! Little did she know she was actually beginning a whole new Career for herself.

The telephone calls were regular but not too frequent and Shirley began to feel much more fulfilled and satisfied with the way she spent the days. Then in mid-December she was invited to join the Steering Committee of We Care, when she questioned 'Why?' she was told because she had done such a good job of filling out her Volunteer Reports. Unsure how Joe would feel about her going to a meeting at night (especially after his earlier misgivings) she was pleased to hear him say it was great how she was making new friends. So that evening she drove to the home of one of the members where many were gathered. There were the members she had spoken to with questions, as well as the new members, like herself, who were just coming aboard. Although it was difficult noting that most of the 'old' and 'new' members seemed to know one another, she never was made to feel left out. The new Chairman was introduced: a priest from the Morris Catholic Church. Shirley knew he was a priest as he had to leave early to hear confessions, but that was all she really noticed, being kept busy writing down all the information she was getting from the others. A short time after Christmas one evening, the phone rang and Shirley was taken by surprise to hear it was that priest calling. He said he would like for her to consider being his Secretary. Shocked, Shirley responded: "But Father, I'm not a Catholic!" He chuckled and explained he meant for the Steering Committee of We Care. "Oh . . . but why ME? I'm new to the community." Father answered by saying he too was new to the community and besides, she was the only one taking notes!" Embarrassed, Shirley explained: "Only because I can't remember things!" With a smile in his voice, he quickly responded: "Ah, see? You're honest too! Please, think about it, won't you? You can call me at this number. Have a pleasant evening. 'Bye!" Stunned, she hung up the wall phone and slowly walked into the living room where all were watching TV.

Once the three youngsters were all in bed, Shirley sat in the quiet house, waiting for Joe to return home from the late shift. Because he was putting in such long hours, sometimes 12-hour days, she waited up for him on these nights so they could have time to talk. Unsure whether or not she wanted to bring up the subject of taking on the responsibility of Secretary, she did what she always did. She turned it over to God, asking that He help her make the right decision. When Joe got home that night he was in a very good mood and happy to relate that the extra hours would soon be a thing of the past. He would be back to working the rotating shift as he had before they'd moved to Morris. That meant so much more time together as a family, plus those 'long weekends' once a month when they could go to the nearby campground where they had become members. Shirley smiled her happiness at the thought, then without preamble she told him of Father's call and his request. "Well, of course you should take it! Those people recognize a good worker when they see one!" Beaming at her husband, she laughed at his words but it was decided that she would go forward with this new opportunity to reach out to others. Lord knows, she thought, she knew what it was to be hurting financially, who could be more qualified?!

The first meeting of the Steering Committee was an interesting one. One of the new members, a woman in her mid seventies, simply announced that first of all, she wasn't a Catholic and secondly she was too old to call this young priest "Father" so what was his answer to that?! Everyone seated around the table held their breath, waiting to see what reaction would result. Father glanced around the table, then with a broad grin responded by saying: "You're right! Why don't you ALL simply call me JR? Those are my initials and most of my friends do just that" . . . and so it went. They were a very compatible group. The group of people who had begun We Care were from Morris, and members of assorted congregations. They had gone to Elgin for a presentation by a clergyman who explained how FISH worked. After they watched his film and listened to his words he opened it up to questions. One of the queries was the name FISH—what did those letters stand for? he was asked. It was explained that back in Biblical times the only way one would identify themselves as a Christian, was by drawing a fish in the sand with their staff. The fish has long been a Christian symbol, hence: the name FISH. So, it was asked, does that name have to be used? No, you can use any name you desire. On returning to Morris the name given was: "We Care For Morris". After this, any calls for help that came through the Police Department or any Church was turned over to the Phone Volunteer on duty at that time, they having a copy of the Volunteer Calendar.

JR conducted the meetings in the Rectory of the church, and because he was a very organized person felt that there should be more structure to this Program. In the past, the only meeting held was an annual one, throughout the year different Committee members kept in touch with the Volunteers and the problems by simply phoning one another. Where did the money come from to buy a meal or put gasoline in a vehicle? Members would simply call other church members and get donations as needed! Even though it was 1973, and this was a small community, it amazed Shirley that they could have carried out their mission in such a flimsy way it went against her organized way of thinking too. JR asked Shirley if she would accompany him the next day to the Morris Police Department as well as a few other places to see if things couldn't be accomplished in a more organized manner. So it began. They made a good team, going to the Ministerial Association which met monthly and was comprised of clergy from all denominations in Morris. The services We Care offered was explained, and the procedure to be followed as well. If anyone came to their particular church seeking help of any kind they were to call the We Care number. In this way one organization would be aware of whom was helped and there would be no duplication of services. The We Care telephone was lodged in the Morris Police Department so they would also be aware of any new individuals seeking help, however, We Care would pay it's own 'phone bill so as not to be a burden on the city. It was a working solution for both We care and the Police. Everyone was cooperating, and it looked like all would be well, when JR was moved to another church! At the meeting when he made his announcement it was assumed that Shirley would take the reins. Quite an assumption, yet what else could she do, she thought? What had been accomplished in such a short time would all go by the wayside if someone didn't head it up. No one else on the committee felt they had the time, the knowledge, "Shirley you must take over!" they insisted, as one. So began the next step of the journey she had embarked on. She contacted the Morris Township Supervisor and asked to hold a meeting in his office. She invited members of the five larger churches to come together to work on establishing Food Pantries for those in need of food. One individual would be called and they would work internally with their members to dole out the food as needed. Shirley set up an Alphabetical system, so families could only go to the Pantry they were sent to by We Care, yet another way to avoid duplication that had occurred in the past. Meanwhile, Shirley made the circuit of Service Clubs: Rotary, Lions, Kiwanis, etc., giving a presentation and receiving a check for a few hundred dollars, which allowed the needs to be met. One night at a Lions dinner she was asked why she didn't go to the United Fund for help, instead of going to these different Service organizations? Shirley looked blankly at the gentleman, and asked what did he mean? Yes, she knew of the United Fund, even remembered when it was called the Community Chest. In fact, she added, her husband had always had a percentage taken from his paycheck to go toward the charity but what did that have to do with her? With the needs of We Care? Patiently, he explained she could go before the Board and request becoming one of the Agencies supported by Grundy County United Fund. She could?! She anxiously asked how that could become possible, and was told simply make an appearance, as long as We Care was incorporated (as a non-profit Agency) it might not be a difficult task at all. About that time, her heart sank, because of course, We Care was NOT incorporated, it was a group of caring individuals doing the best they could to help anyone in need. The idea was planted that night, but unknown to Shirley a terrible piece of news was soon to arrive that would devastate the entire family.

It had been five years living in Morris, much had happened in that time. During one of many telephone calls Judy admitted to a failing marriage. Her dream of a 'perfect' marriage with the 'perfect' man was failing rapidly. At last on June 27, 1978 the marriage ended in divorce, after nine years and three children. Although she thought she could make it as a single parent, the struggle was almost impossible, until at last she turned over the custody of the children to her ex-husband for as long as it took to 'get on her feet' financially. Although she was 'invited' to come to Morris she refused as she wanted to stay in Carpentersville, where she 'hoped to work things out' but that was not to be. On the 3rd of October of that year, she was found in a rustic motel, in a nearby township, deceased. A suicide letter addressed to John, her ex-husband, was next to her on the bed. In it she once more declared her love for him and the children. She begs him to 'make them understand their mommy loves them.' That evening Joe was in the kitchen putting on his work shoes and Shirley was on the couch in the living room, when suddenly the front door opened and in came John and Jim with their wives, with Joyce and her husband. A shocked Shirley looked up with a "Whaaat" on her lips, as Joyce knelt in front of her. With tear glistened eyes she looked into Shirley's and said: "Mom, Judy is gone." Completely befuddled Shirley asked: "Where? Where has she—" Then from the kitchen she heard Joe's howl of pain. Heard him saying: "no, No, Oh, God, NO!!" And she knew.

After the funeral, it was a difficult time for everyone. Joe had to return to work, as did Jerry, while Julie and Joey went back to school. This, of course, left Shirley alone to deal with her thoughts and sadness. She came to realize how much a suicide affects so many people. She recalled when the children were young she used to bring them to a park in Elgin where there was a pond and stream, where they loved to throw rocks. One day, on impulse she explained how when one pebble tossed into a quiet body of water could create circle after circle so could each person touch other lives. Remembering that time now, she thought it the same with suicide, it reached out to so many causing one to blame themselves. To wonder if there was one more thing they might have said or done. To wonder if there was one more thing they shouldn't have said or done. She reached out to the Bible Jude had left behind and as she opened it a paper fluttered out. Frowning she reached out to recover it, and there, in Judy's handwriting, was a request to have the 23rd Psalm read when she died so family and friends might remember her by it! In her other hand she held the "In Remembrance" card from the funeral parlor that she had been about to insert in its pages. There, printed in gold letters was the 23rd Psalm! Instead of more weeping she took a deep breath feeling calm at last, after being unable to draw a breath for what seemed so long. It felt as though Judy reached out from her grave to reassure her the family had truly done their best by her. It was the real beginning of healing for Shirley and she knew she'd be able to reassure the rest of the family, knowing Judy was at rest at last, free from the world she could no longer face.

Later that month Joe was being sent to the University of Wisconsin for Supervisory Training and suggested Shirley accompany him. When she said she couldn't possibly go, he said she could. A weekend away would be good for her, being gone for two nights and a day Jerry, now 21, was certainly more than capable of taking care of things, plus Julie, 17, Joey 15, were no longer young children. So it was decided, they would leave Friday and return Sunday afternoon. As she began to pack for two days Shirley thought this may actually be another gift from God. She began to look forward to what she would do while Joe attended day classes. She would take advantage of the University Library and with plenty of free time to work on finding how We Care could become incorporated! This would be her dedication to Judy, she would reach out to help other young people to veer from the path Judy chose. She did just that, and on returning to Morris made an appointment with the City Attorney. Armed with all the notes she had taken, she explained her dilemma and he was more than reassuring. He agreed to walk her through the entire process . . . pro bono! Yet another prayer answered, Shirley thought as she began an ever surer walk out of his office and into her future.

Once incorporated as a non-profit agency, the United Fund Board granted her a hearing and she found herself speaking before these prominent individuals. Standing at the podium, notes before her, she stated her case as simply as possible. Her concern, she said, was that she had been working out of her home these past five years and all the files she kept there in a cabinet. What would happen if she and her husband were in an accident? There would be no way her protective children would allow anyone to go into their home to retrieve those files! She was requesting monetary assistance so that she might have an actual office where all information could be kept. The Morris Post Master had offered her a place in the upper level of the Post Office. The Board granted her the annual request and she was able to obtain a desk, and other office needs. This, of course meant having to go into said office daily, yet it was a good way to concentrate on any business to come her way. The telephone was incorporated into the City Police Board, so while We Care offered services 24/7 there was always an alert voice to answer any call. If Shirley was needed the Police would contact her at home or office. She began to carry a beeper at that time so as not to miss any calls. We Care was getting more and more calls for help. Shirley felt needed more than ever, not just by her husband or her children, but by individuals within the County. When the corporate papers were drawn up Shirley had named the organization: "We Care Of Grundy County, Inc." extending help throughout the county rather than containing it to Morris, only. She had become recognized and accepted by all, as a caring individual, willing to help in any and all situations. There was a Clothes Closet, with clothing donated by local persons and 'manned' by two Volunteer women. One Volunteer man created shelving and hanging places in the room donated by the local Nursing

Home. Many were given clothes in different circumstances: The semi-driver whose truck had skidded on the ice over I-80 surface and overturned. The injured driver was a tall Texan who was hospitalized. Told he could be released the following day he realized all his belongings were in the semi which had been towed by the company that owned it. He had need of a complete outfit to get back to his job, but he still had his boots, he reassured Shirley when she spoke with him. After a visit to the closet she was able to bring all the needed items to him, and he was most grateful, if a little embarrassed, but was reassured that there was no need for that. He was most welcome. Usually the calls came from a school within the county, for a child needing winter coats or boots, these needs too, were met. One morning Shirley had just got to the office when the We Care phone rang as she entered. Tired, having been called out of bed at 2 a.m. for a young couple stranded at the nearby truck stop, Shirley answered the call to find it was the couple she had put up into a local motel earlier that morning. Calling them back at the motel, they told of their need for winter clothes, especially the young woman. They had come from a warm state, to a cold, March day in Illinois. Obtaining sizes Shirley went to the Closet and was able to find a man-made 'fur' coat in her size, but only heavy sweaters for her husband. Driving to the motel, Shirley was granted entrance, where she heard the sad story they had to tell. He had just been released from the Army, was still in his uniform and she, a young little thing of 19, wore sandals and a thin summer dress. They were on the way to her grandmothers' where a job awaited him, and housing was taken care of. They had accepted the offer of a ride with neighbors the wife had met. This couple, (described as 'older' could have been in their 30's and considered 'older' by these youngsters Shirley thought), had offered a ride if the soldier would help with the driving. However, about midnight the night before, they pulled into the parking lot of a nearby truck stop, where the man took the soldier aside. He was told to go into the restaurant and ask for money to help him on his way, but the young man said he was unable to do that. He was a soldier, in uniform, and would not disgrace it! Angry, the man turned to his wife and told her of his uncooperative attitude, whereupon the woman told the young girl she should go from parked truck to truck and 'earn' a few dollars! Of course the newlywed refused, then asked if she would sell her wedding gown she burst into tears, crying "No!" At this point the couple threw all the youngsters belongings onto the lot and drove away, leaving them stranded.

The truck stop owner had called the police and that's how Shirley had gotten involved in getting them into the motel. After reassuring them she could get them a bus ticket to her grandmothers' Shirley was about to leave to accomplish that task, when she told them to get their suitcase together and she would pick them up and drive them to the bus depot, which was at the same truck stop where they'd been left. Crying, the young woman explained she had no suitcase, all her things were in a plastic laundry basket! Once she told them they would have to put these things in boxes or the bus wouldn't let them board—there were more tears. Soon Shirley found herself at the local grocery market where they not only supplied her with a couple of sturdy boxes, but loaned her twine, tape and a marker pen! Back to the motel, leaving these with the couple she got the bus tickets, went back to pick them up and bring them to the truck stop where the bus would be coming within the hour. Smiling, on the receiving end of many hugs, Shirley wished them well and headed back to the office. As she entered her office she once again heard the telephone. Unlocking the door, feeling unusually worried, she reached the phone and answered: "We Care, this is Shirley." Her heart started beating rapidly as she heard the young woman's tearful voice, "Oh, Shirley—we have another problem!" "What happened did you miss the bus? What's wrong? Stop crying, I can't understand you . . ."

Breathing hard, she managed to say: "Its Princess! Jimmy says the trucks can't stop like a car and she could be killed! Can you help?" "Wait—Wait, slow down", Shirley urged, "who is Princess?" Well, seems like Princess was a tiny little kitten that her new husband had given her, and who had been in the laundry basket of clothing when it was tossed out of the car. Of course, the frightened cat had sped off and now, the next day, had reappeared as they sat waiting for the bus! Glancing at the wall clock, seeing she had only about 25 minutes before the bus would arrive, she shouted she'd be right there, and once again tore out of the Post Office building heading for the truck stop! Thinking all the way: "What am I doing? I must be crazy! What am I going to do?!" As she pulled into the lot she had no trouble sighting them, a young soldier with his duffel bag over his shoulder, and his young wife next to him, but her hair seems so long, Shirley thought, irreverently. Then as she pulled along side of them, she realized it wasn't long hair she was seeing but a kitten perched on the shoulder of the young woman in her 'fur' coat. As the girl opened the passenger side door, she leaned in to tell Shirley if she would just take the cat to the vet and have it put to sleep she would be grateful. She just couldn't live with the thought of it being crushed under 18 wheels of a semi! As she spoke these words the kitten disentangled itself, and jumped onto the seat next to Shirley! Looking from the couple to the cat, Shirley saw these lovely green eyes pleading with her, accompanied by the lightest of meows! Having just lost her cat a few weeks earlier, whose name was "Princess" she actually felt her eyes tearing, as she tried to find her voice. Picking up the kitten she promised she would find it a home, not to worry, just get on that bus! Now!! And they did just that, waving to her as they boarded. Driving right to her Vet where she brought her two Yorkie pups, she presented the kitten to him, asking for his opinion on its health. After a thorough check he questioned if she'd had her shots and of course, not knowing for sure, Shirley replied she doubted it as the owner had no money. After getting the shots, Shirley drove home, deciding it was useless to return to the office that day. Soon she entered her home and slowly "introduced" the two dogs to their new little roommate. Both dogs had lived with Princess, her cat, so were delighted to have a new playmate. Not so, with this frightened little kitten! Jumping up on a kitchen stool she perched looking down on them, not at all happy. Because she had the lovely coloring of a Calico Shirley immediately renamed her "Callie", not yet being able to bear hearing the name of 'Princess.' When Joe came home that night imagine his surprise to see this tiny ball of fur, who soon became another loved family member. (Always to be referred to, as their "We Care Cat!")

Just as the Clothing Closet had helped many people, there had once been a small building located on the Methodist Church parking lot. Here canned goods were stored to be given to those in need of food. However, back when R.J. and Shirley made their first trip there, they found that the bug population outnumbered the canned goods. By mutual agreement they emptied it out and disposed of the entire unsanitary mess. It was about this time that R.J. was transferred to another Church and Shirley became the President.

Shirley made the rounds of Morris Churches speaking to the clergy, she explained her idea of creating five Food Panties for those in need in Morris. They were asked to present the idea to their respective congregations and give Shirley the names of two people willing to be their 'Pantry People.' This done, she had everyone meet with her to explain their roles. The result was a well set-up Program whereas the larger congregations would handle those letters of the alphabet most generally in need, the smaller would take the rest. The only way anyone could be serviced by a Pantry was through a referral by We Care, who would be responsible to check out their financial circumstances. This would prevent any "double-dipping" which had occurred in the past, plus We Care would help with the job of obtaining the needed food to stock said Pantry. Different groups held food-raising events, after which the foods were given to We Care to sort. These items would be distributed to the Pantries. As this worked well, she set up Pantries in the other Villages throughout the County. Each of these worked the same way, with referrals from We Care as an only admission.

At this time transportation was still offered to and from medical facilities, at no cost to the client. This was achieved through Transportation Volunteers, who drove their own vehicles. Often husband and wife teams drove to out of town facilities and shopped while the client was at their doctors. The client was then brought back to their own doorstep. The Telephone Volunteers had increased as well, Shirley was thrilled to be able to interact with over 150 Volunteers who served in one or another capacity. There were even some families who offered their own homes for overnight stays in an Emergency situation.

There was the time three youngsters were found walking down I-80 after midnight! The State Police called Shirley at 1 a.m. Could We Care house them until their parents were found? Shirley called one of the names on her list, an elderly widow, who was glad to help out. After being transported to her home the oldest a girl, 12, was shown her room and her two brothers, 7 and 9 theirs. About an hour later the woman was awakened by a strange noise. Using to living alone, she went to investigate. As she passed the rooms where the children were she saw the beds were empty. Turning toward the staircase she felt pressure on her shoulders and as she twisted to see behind her found herself being pushed down the stairs! Painfully getting to her feet she called the police. When they arrived, the children were found upstairs, each holding a pillowcase filled with stolen items! Fortunately the woman was not hurt badly, but suffered heartache to think this could happen . . . they were just children! That morning that particular service was no longer in existence.

As years passed Shirley reconciled her feelings for her mother, and phone her each weekend to inquire as to her health. They had established a relationship once again, then, in 1987 circumstances changed radically. Due to poor health Rose came to live with Joe and Shirley in March of that year. After many months of seeking her health records from her Chicago doctor, establishing her with a Morris doctor, she began to be her old self once again. Still weak, but gaining strength, through good meals at regular times, as well as medication ordered by her doctor. As time passed, though, her mental state began to get worse, and then there were physical problems. Two years later, on December 3, 1989 she passed away and was buried next to her husband.

One day in December of 1981, Shirley got a call from one of her elderly clients, Francis. She was quite distraught, feeling ill, and unable to decide if she should be taken to the hospital. Attempting to calm her down, Shirley questioned her as to what exactly had happened. "Well" Francis explained: "this really nice man and his friends insisted on taking me to the Holiday Inn for a special pre-Christmas dinner and maybe, maybe it was really my own fault, but I ate a lot of things I'm not supposed to!" Shirley smiled to herself and promised she'd come right over. Bagging a bottle of Pepto Bismo she did just that. A couple of tablespoons later she had Francis relaxing over a cup of tea, relating how "this nice man" had come into her life. It seemed he was an official at a local bank where she kept her account, and he was aware she subsisted on Social Security alone. He had explained how he and his group of friends had gotten together after Church services and recognizing how fortunate they were, decided to reach out to someone *less* so, to make their Christmastime a little brighter. She (Francis) had been the one they decided upon, would she allow them to do this for her? Overwhelmed by such generosity by strangers, she had accepted their offer. The group of three couples treated her to a special dinner, as well as desert, urging her to eat and enjoy. Problem was, Francis was diabetic as well as on a special diet and as a result, she couldn't sleep that night as well as feeling poorly this morning. Once Shirley was assured she would be alright, she helped her into bed and left on a vendetta to really chew "that nice man" out!

A short time later, Shirley walked into the bank and searched out "the nice man", by the name Francis had given her: 'Joe S." Barging into where angels fear to tread, she began to read the poor man the riot act! Taken aback, he looked shocked at this woman he did not even know! As she explained how he and his friends had taken Francis out as a 'treat' it turned out to have poor results. As she finally paused for breath Joe jumped in and asked her who she was?! Are you her relative? Her daughter? Shirley answered that she was her client. "Client? What, are you a lawyer then?" At last, realizing she had probably gone overboard, Shirley introduced herself as the Administrator of We Care and Francis was a client, as well as a dear friend of many years. Staring at her, an open-mouthed Joe asked and what is 'We Care'? So began what would be the beginning of a friendship that would last many years. As she explained that if Joe and his friends had money to help someone have a 'nice Christmas' she could put them in touch with individuals or families who were in true need. She had begun a Program she'd named: "Adopt A Family" and through this Program was able to assist many, many families throughout the County. She explained that $100 could be used for a family rather than an individual! (In 1982 a family of four could buy enough groceries for a special dinner plus for $25!) She explained "the rules" were for each family to receive just that, plus at least one COMPARABLE gift per child, to be delivered by the persons or group who does the 'adopting.' Intrigued by the whole idea Joe told Shirley he would be in touch with her after Christmas.

True to his word, Joe called Shirley in January and they discussed the possibility of working toward having a 'Community Dinner' on Christmas Day for any families who might not otherwise have one. Shirley was to assemble the families, and Joe and his friends would purchase one gift per child as she got a wish list from the parents! This came after other meetings some of which occurred in the local KFC where they lunched and talked. As the ideas were thrown around the then-Manager, Mark B. approached them. He said he couldn't help but overheard their discussion and he would like to offer KFC as the location! They were closed to the public on Christmas he explained, but after speaking to his employees (mostly young people) they volunteered to work that day for the few hours the Dinner would last. While grateful for such an offer, Shirley explained they really wanted a full turkey dinner with all the fixings . . . not chicken. Ah, but his distributor could probably get turkeys he answered. At the next meeting they were given even more amazing news! Once he explained about the Community Dinner the distributor agreed to deliver the turkeys, at no charge! Joe and Shirley continued to exchange smiles, knowing God's hands were truly involved in this. It was no longer an idea or a dream but come Christmas it would be a reality!

On Christmas Day, 1982, by noon there were gathered together some thirteen families, with thirty four child present. (Two families were unable to attend, one had her mother hospitalized and other had a death in the family, so their children's gifts were brought to their home that afternoon.) All those workers gave of themselves, worked at serving a delicious meal. As Shirley spoke with the families she overheard the workers asking if the folks would like foil to take home their leftovers. At one point potential customers arrived, thinking the restaurant was open for business, as everyone held their breath Mark simply opened the door to say: "We're closed, really sorry but this is a PRIVATE PARTY!" Everyone breathed sighs of relief, exchanging smiles with one another. Then, suddenly there were bells jingling and Santas' ho ho ho's were heard throughout the room, and all thirty four big-eyed children froze in place! Enthralled, as Santa entered! He sat in a special chair and called each child by name, and hand delivered each beautifully wrapped gift, marked with that child's name. There were Leggo's, doll's, games and more. There were many happy tears shed that day. In her job as Administrator, Shirley dealt with people daily, mostly those who had problems. This one Christmas Day, for a couple of hours she saw this large group of people forget their problems. She saw joy and hope and love in their eyes, a beautiful sight. On returning home that day, Shirley told Joe she had to go in her office and write thanks you's right there and then, while the emotions were still at their highest. Because she did just that, Joe called her and was so thrilled at her descriptions that once again she heard: "We've got to meet!"

Meet they did. Joe wanted so mulch to witness the miracles Shirley had described that once again ideas were exchanged. How to make it bigger. How to include even more people. Then, the then-Manager of the local radio station, Terry, came and joined them. Ideas were flowing as Terry agreed to two of them really were on the right track. But he felt a name was needed for his group. A name? Why? Because, Terry explained, I have a great idea on how you could raise funds. You could have one annual auction over the radio so others in the community might be involved in helping their neighbors in need. That day the name Operation St. Nick was born. The first radio auction was held that year and through a quirk of fate Joe was able to come into possession of a most wanted item: Cabbage Patch Dolls! The auction was on the air from 11 a.m. til noon on a Sunday. People called in and bid on the doll, starting at $100. A local businessman finally outbid the others with the amount of $895!! The story actually was picked up by AP wires. The Annual Radio Auction was born that day, and it too was destined to grow.

That year of 1983 $6,403 was raised and 37 families with 143 people were helped with clothing, food and gifts. The Dinner was moved to the Morris Holiday Inn, complete with a decorated tree, a fireplace with a plush chair beside it, begging to be filled by St. Nick! But, so as not to be left out of the festivities, it was catered by KFC! That Friday evening, December 23, there were 90 guests, made up of 63 children and their parents. Again, tears of joy, hugs, and thanks! As years passed the methods of yearly celebrations changed, but the results were always wonderful and the number of families increased as the donations continued to grow. The success of Operation St. Nick is truly an Impossible Dream! How in this small rural county of Grundy such huge sums could come is impossible, yet happened. More and more became involved by having their own fund raisers and donating it to OSN. As more money became available more Programs were added. Easter became a time to give assistance to those in need. Then Shirley saw the need through We Care, that families were having with school supplies. In 1997 The Back to School Program was born where children were given their supplies plus a new outfit and gym needs. This soon became a very important part of students lives and OSN was a proud provider. In 2002 St. Nick won the Hometown Award and went to Springfield, IL to accept the aware presented by Illinois State Treasurer, Judy Barr Topinka. Operation St. Nick is a very important part in the lives of Joe and Shirley and probably always will be a legacy for them both. In the year 2010 a milestone figure of $109,330 was raised at the December 5 Radio Auction! A true

Million Dollar moment! The Impossible Dream had really become Possible! So the families in need in Grundy County will continue to be assisted as long as such community generosity goes on.

Meanwhile, as Shirley's life became more involved in the workings of St. Nick and her daily work with We Care changes were taking place at home too. There was the afternoon Joe returned home from work and putting his lunchbox on the counter told Shirley the terrible news he had been 'let go' from his job. It was more of a shock to him then he could believe. He was closing in on retirement age and it was going to be expensive for him to be kept on, so he was 'given' several weeks of pay as were several of his co-workers in the same age bracket. Shameful treatment for a man who had always given his all, but there was no recourse. The next day Shirley told Joe they should go to the Unemployment Agency so he could sign up until he could find some kind of job. He immediately told her there was no need to hurry because he had been 'given' all these weeks of salary! "No! You were not 'given' anything, you got what you earned and not near what you deserved," Shirley informed him! "We'll go to Ottawa tomorrow and sign up." Upset, Joe told her he couldn't go to Ottawa he had to go to Joliet like the other guys had. They had told him stories of the long lines he would need to endure, and he was not anxious to go. Patiently, Shirley explained that he could, indeed, go to Ottawa, and the lines were short if even existent. "What do you know about it?" Joe growled? "I know plenty about it" she retorted. "What do you think I do at We Care? The many men who lost their jobs at the paper mill were men who had to be taken through the whole process, and we learned together. Trust me, this is my job!" Shirley had always declared that "some good comes from whatever bad happens" and perhaps this was another such situation. The next morning an unbelieving Joe walked into an empty unemployment office where he and Shirley were treated to smiling workers who had them on their way in less than a half hour! What was the "good"? Well, at long last Joe began to respect the Job Shirley did. He had simply looked upon it as her keeping busy so as not to be bored. He really had little knowledge of the inner workings, the accomplishments, simply because he had never asked and wasn't too interested! Yes, he had attended each Annual Meeting where Shirley had met with and thanked all the many Volunteers, but he had never really taken her seriously until the day her knowledge affected him.

As it turned out, the current President of her We Care Board was a young man in charge of a Workshop for the mentally disabled who was seeking a person to take over as Manager. He asked Joe if he'd be interested and to Shirley's surprise—he was! Knowing how sentimental and soft hearted he could be, Shirley questioned if he could handle such a job. As it worked out, he loved working with those clients, and they in turn, loved him! He remained there until he felt the time came when he should retire. He was in reasonably good health and loved playing golf so he thought he would enjoy the free time, asking Shirley if she would think about retiring as well. Shirley gave in to where she hired someone to work with her, in 1989. The We Care office had moved to the back part of the Township building which gave them adequate office space for two, but a large area where they could accept the foods collected by many organizations. Shirley loved her job, helping people had become such an important part of her life, she dreaded giving it up, but she trained Deb so she might take over—eventually.

Her family had undergone many changes over the years. Jerry had moved back to the Dundee area to seek employment. Julie had married a Morris man and began her own life, while Joe, after graduation, attended Bradley College. So the Empty Nest Syndrome was in full force and Shirley and Joe spent many wonderful hours together. While she spent the day in the We Care office he was golfing and reaching out to make many new men friends, all was well with the world!

For her 70th Birthday, Shirley conceived the idea of what she thought would be a great fundraiser for We Care! Having had a "List of things to do—before I die" the one thing she had never done was to jump from a plane in a free fall! Having taken many parachute "rides" in Riverview Park, as a Chicago teen, she savored the idea of the 'real' thing! Going to Hawaii had topped the list, and been achieved. Going white-water rafting had its appeal, they'd done that, as well, but the Skydiving? Not yet, she thought. So after contacting Morris Airport to be told by the owner of Skydive, would donate the jump because it was to benefit We Care, things began to fall in place. Next came a doctor's visit where she had an EKG and stress test, just taking precautions, and an OK from her unbelieving physician followed. Although Joe couldn't see why she wanted to do it, he stood behind her in the decision. Her children were all very supportive and soon the entire community became involved.

The Sunday before her Birthday all the family came to Morris to honor Shirley on Mothers' Day. Everyone looked forward to the following Saturday when the Skydiving would take place. That day was very uncooperative, weather-wise! The winds were too high and the clouds too low and the jump was canceled! What a major disappointment! Most of the city was in attendance, hundreds were let down, but not as much as Shirley, who had raised $5,418. for her cause! Still, the family had one more day to be together, which was something to hang on to, she thought. The jump had been postponed until the following Saturday which would be her actual Birthday; 5/29/28.

On Friday evening of 5/28/98 Joe and Shirley joined 16 friends from their Church for dinner at a local restaurant. The group was known as "50 plus" and was composed of members in that age category. The evening was a combined dinner/ meeting and was a wonderful time of fellowship. Because they had ridden with another couple they invited these friends in for a few hours of playing cards, which the four had often done in the past. Once their guests had left, Shirley and Joe retired for the evening. Around 5 a.m. Shirley was awakened by Joe calling her . . . half asleep she made her way to the bathroom where she found Joe sitting on the closed stool, hanging onto the basin. "What is it?" she asked. "What's wrong?" Looking up he told her he had been vomiting blood, but as she looked into the sink and saw none, she surmised it must have been tomato sauce, as they'd dined on Italian food the night before. She started to say this, when Joe interrupted her and said she'd better call an ambulance. Shirley felt such shock! Her years of answering the We Care 'phone in the wee hours, came to the fore and she ran to her desk, picked up the business phone which was connected to the Morris Police Board. She told the dispatcher what Joe had just said and he responded by telling her to "get dressed" he had just dispensed an ambulance. Never questioning, she ran back to Joe, told him the ambulance was on the way she was going to get dressed, could he hold on? He nodded, and she ran to get into her clothes. Soon the EMT's were running up their driveway with equipment in hand. A close friend/ neighbor appeared at the door while they worked on Joe, and Shirley asked her to call her Pastor and her son, Joe, who could call his sister Julie. Once they had Joe on a gurney headed down the drive, Shirley called out she would see him in the hospital, and he answered with an: 'Okay'. Following the ambulance she arrived at the hospital only to be told she would have to sign some papers before she could see him.

When Joe had answered her with his 'Okay' it was to be the last time she would ever hear his voice. Her love of 38 years died on the table that early morning (5:30 a.m.) of her 70th Birthday! Soon, her friend John, the Coroner, arrived to find her in tears while speaking on the telephone at the nurses' station. Standing next to her, literally holding her up, was her son, Joe. He, along with her Pastor had accompanied her to see Joe lying, unmoving, gone forever. As she returned to the waiting room where many had already gathered, she had been summoned to the 'phone where a person from the Organ Donor's organization was seeking information. John took her other arm and led her way with her son. That scene was never to be repeated as John worked toward a method whereby no other newly widowed person would be subjected to such cold, uncaring type questioning.

Soon Shirley found herself at home, surrounded by family and caring friends, the Sky Dive forgotten, now a thing of the past, never to be attained. Nothing seemed important anymore.

Jerry and Linda had sold their Carpentersville home and most of their belongings were on the road heading toward their new home in Phoenix, AZ. When they received the call that Joe was in the hospital. None of the children were advised of his death until their arrival in Morris. Jerry drove to his mothers' home to be shocked, along with his siblings, at this sudden turn of events. All their clothing being shipped, they faced buying clothes for a funeral! They stayed with Shirley throughout the next days, keeping her spirits up as best they could. Soon though, they and everyone else had to get back to their own lives, and it was then that Shirley faced reality once again! This time alone!

In 1997 Shirley was thrilled to learn the judges chose her for the 1997 Senior Citizen of Grundy County Award. Now, in 1998, she worried what direction her life should take—should she forget her plans to retire from We Care? Should she submerge herself as she did when she lost her daughter, Judy? When Deb took over the reins of We Care changes began, with her family she felt unable to continue with the Emergency Service hours. No longer in the Police System, the Agency became a 9 to 5 position. Closed on weekends and Holiday pay was given. In January of 2001 she retired as Administrator, leaving We Care in what she felt were able hands. Although she chose to stay on the Board, it was startling for Shirley to see more and more changes as time went by. In January of 2006, Shirley was saddened to find that Deb was submitting her resignation stating that the demands of the job didn't allow for her to be with family, especially during the Holidays. So began the We Care Board's search for a new leader, which eventually culminating in the hiring of Denise. Shortly after Shirley felt it time, after 35 years, to retire from the We Care Board as well, and so ended that Era of her life. Not entirely, though, she would come to discover.

As Shirley continued with her life, sans We Care, she was never bored nor without something to do! She continued with her other Volunteer obligations: Chairman of Crime Stoppers of Grundy County, Chairman of the State's Attorneys Justice Assistance Board, Secretary of the 100 Club of Grundy County, President of the Morris Senior Center all took her away from home, In 2001 she was presented with the Key to the City of Morris by then, Mayor Feeney, something she treasured as the first and only recipient!

In the year of 2002 she received the Women of Achievement Award from Lieutenant Governor Corinne Wood. She had been nominated for the honor by Morris Mayor Richard Kopczick for this state-level recognition. So recently after her retirement as We Care Administrator this was an unexpected reward for doing what she considered her 'job' which took place in Chicago at the James R. Thompson Center.

In 2008 she was invited to lunch by Denise and still President of the We Care Board, Dave. When she arrived she was surprised that Joe (her co-worker with Operation St. Nick) was also seated at the table. Slowly she sank into the chair held out for her, looking from one to the other, all smiling at her, she blurted: "What is going on? What are you three up to?" Laughing, they explained their mission. In the beginnings of We Care Shirley had worked from her home, then after years of renting office space and enduring four moves they had been given an opportunity to buy its current office space! They felt that under her direction it had grown from a fledgling provider to volunteer service into a nonprofit corporation with the means to help thousands of Grundy County families throughout the years. They were proposing a fundraiser which would honor her on her 80th Birthday, by naming the new office "The Shirley Kiss Center". Stunned, not able to grasp all this, she began by explaining she wouldn't be able to take part in a Radio-thon on that Sunday, as her children were hosting an open house for her to celebrate. She was surprised to be told that her children had already been contacted, advised and were thrilled with the idea! So all area residents were urged to call into the local radio station June 1st to pledge to help We Are raise the needed $80,000! (That figure was given by Jim and Carol Baum who had purchased the entire building to be developed—in honor of her 80th Birthday.) So Joe and Shirley were on the air on both AM and FM stations from 9 a.m. until noon. People came in and telephone messages and stories were shared about Shirley and continued on at the VFW where her Birthday Party began at 1 p.m. Sunday started off with $4,965 already received by mailings to We Care prior to Shirley Kiss Day. (So named by both the City of Morris, as well as the Grundy County Board, and proclaimed on a huge banner hung on the wall of the VFW building!) By time noon rolled around, the donations totaled $42,000! More than half of the needed sum. When Shirley arrived at the VFW she was nearly overwhelmed by the huge number of people who came and went throughout the afternoon. Her children had all taken part in the decorations, each family prepared a large Bulletin Board Display of special events in their family in which she had been a part of with many photos. There were balloons, M&M's with her name, candy Kisses' not to mention the luncheon which had been catered. There were two 6-foot tables covered with all the many plaques she'd been awarded over the years. A large Book titled 'The Life of Shirley Kiss' was presented by her son, Jim. All family members were dressed in orange shirts with "Celebration of Life" printed across the front in white. In all, it was indeed a celebration, and as it so happened, June 1st was the only day available for this party, and so the date of May 29th wasn't mentioned to damper the spirits of everyone. After the long, exhausting but uplifting day, Shirley went to bed with a prayer that Joe had witnessed it all, and was proud and happy for her.

The following year the beautiful sign, hand-painted, was hung on the building during a beautiful recognition ceremony. Shirley was stunned to see an Angel painted atop her name, and questioned Denise. With a smile Denise explained how Shirley had told Debbi and many others, over the years that she had an Angel over her desk. It was the only explanation she could come up with, as to why things worked out so well. When a call would come for a specific needed item; refrigerator, washer, bed, whatever, it would only be a matter of a day or two and that item was offered as a donation! What else could it be but an Angel? She'd reasoned. Hence the angel! Shirley smiled in return.

Shirley went on about her life, remaining active in Community affairs, and the many organizations she'd belonged to for so long. One day she began putting up Fall decorations, both inside and outdoors, as she always had. While putting together some of the foliage she thought she should create a decoration for Joe's headstone. She drove out to the cemetery and removed the summer flowers putting the fall ones in. Struggling to arrange the grouping so it looked as nice as possible she carried on yet another conversation with Joe, telling him how she'd done the house as he used to say he enjoyed. Soon finished, she strolled over to the car where she'd left the engine running and the radio playing. As she looked across the car's roof she realized she had not said a prayer, but of course she HAD talked to him, but—Still, she slid into the drivers seat and as she did, the radio began playing "Pretty Woman". She literally sank into the seat, rather stunned, but she knew! Joe had always played that song for her from when they first dated in the 60's. So she smiled and said aloud, looking at the headstone: "You're welcome, honey!" and drove back home, comforted and ready for whatever the future might hold.

EPILOGUE

AS I FINISH what I started many years ago, I can't help but add a few thoughts that have come to mind. I feel no one who believes in God (as I do) should fear death. I am more 'afraid' of what I might not accomplish if I die tomorrow. I remember back one Sunday when Joe and I just returned from Church and were discussing the Pastor's sermon. It was centered on 'being ready' and Joe looked directly at me and said: "Well, you know I'm ready." Taken aback I quickly said: "Well, I'm not!" Joe laughed and said: "Shirley you'll never be ready, you always have 'one more thing to do' why, you can't just sit and watch TV with me, you have a book on your lap, or doing your nails, you can't seem to just sit." I think of that now, and realize he was right, I feel there is so much still undone. I find comfort in knowing he was ready and some guilt in knowing I do seem always to be planning ahead. I really wanted to finish this story of my life, for those I'll leave behind, so they might come to know me as a person not only their mom, grandmother, etc. That I made mistakes along the way but that my love for each of them never swayed and continues to this very moment. I know I'm extremely fortunate to have survived the abusive times of my life and lived to see my children become adults. That had been an oft-repeated prayer in the past. Now, to be so blessed to see their choice of life-partners, and those who have become parents do so in a loving way. This fills me with great joy and gratefulness to God, to know the abuse was never passed on. As I've aged I have seen my grandchildren grow, marry, and have children of their own! This fills me with indescribable happiness. I am truly blessed.

To have been fortunate enough to have been given so many opportunities in life—to be put into the position to be able to reach out and help those in need, those who have suffered abuse. This has been a dream come true. We Care allowed for me to put my own bad experiences to good use. Allowed me to be compassionate and able to truly understand what they were suffering through in their lives. I sincerely believe God placed me in Grundy County for the sole purpose of reaching out, and I'm grateful to have been His tool through We Care and whatever other means. What an honor it has been. When a client told of how their drug use was 'because my parents/siblings did it,' or 'I abuse my spouse/children because that's what my father did' etc. I am happy to have proved what I told one client after another: "You must be who you are IN SPITE OF, NOT BECAUSE OF." Because I, who had no self esteem as a young person, was gifted by God to be able to accomplish so much for so many, in spite of the verbal abuse in my youth and the physical abuse as an adult. I am grateful to God, for my life, and will be ready when God calls me home.

Shirley I. Kiss